BASIC COMPOSITION:

A STEP-BY-STEP APPROACH

LOUISE DEFELICE

New Readers Press
Publishing Division of Laubach Literacy International
Syracuse, New York

Dedication

This book is dedicated to all my students who have taught me so much and especially to:

Mary	Ollie	Paul	Keith	Fred
John	Shirley	Larry	Debbie	Walter
"Zeke"	Glenn	Elaine	Terry	Algernon
Musallam	Bob	Trenay	Julian	Kelsey

Acknowledgements

I am grateful to Ms. Juanita Gray who planted the seeds of this book many years ago and to Mrs. Barbara Giordano for the valuable suggestions which helped to refine my ideas. Also, a very special thank you to Dr. Edward M. O'Keefe and Mrs. Carol Jelinek for their help and encouragement.

Material quoted in Chapter 1 by Ernest Hemingway, excerpted from *A Moveable Feast*. Copyright © 1964 Mary Hemingway. Reprinted with the permission of Charles Scribner's Sons.

Cover photo: Comstock, Inc./
Tom Grill

ISBN 0-88336-362-3

Revised Edition

First Edition, Let's Do It—Write

EACH ONE TEACH ONE

Printed in the United States of America
Project Editor: Christina M. Jagger
Editor: Mary Hutchison
Cover design by: Chris Steenwerth

9 8 7 6 5 4 3 2 1

Table of Contents

Introduction

The longest journey begins with the first step. Surprise!! You've already taken the first step in solving the mysteries of writing. You've opened this book and begun to read. No one made fun of you. Your heart didn't stop beating, nor did the earth tremble. It was no big deal. The first step was painless.

The rest of the journey is painless as well. I didn't say it was easy. I said it was painless. Your journey will require some work. You will begin by unlocking the magical universe you have inside you. You will explore the unique world of ideas and impressions which make up the special way you think and feel—those things that are inside your head but that you haven't always been able to express in writing.

Writing demands that you think, and thinking means that you will both explore and organize those fragments of ideas and insights you have inside your head. Writing will enable you to organize them into a form that will help to make sense of what's going on inside you. It will also help others see what you see, feel what you feel, and understand what you are thinking.

You're on your way. Don't turn back. This is an important journey for you. It will reward you with knowledge about yourself and the pleasure that comes from being able to share your ideas, insights, and opinions with others.

As you progress on this journey, you will also learn that you can make just as good an impression on paper as you make in person when you are at your best. Writing represents us on paper. This is one of the reasons we are so squeamish about writing. Instead of being able to appear in person to present our ideas, we are represented only by our words on a piece of paper.

Most of us try to look our best when we expect to meet other people. But when we express ourselves on paper and our writing skills are not the best, our appearance on paper doesn't match the carefully groomed individuals we are in person. Instead of creating a good impression, we can end up making a bad impression. As we work to improve our writing, we learn to present our ideas well on paper. In other words, the *us* on paper comes closer and closer to matching the *us* in person.

To achieve all this requires some risk on your part. You'll have to risk making mistakes, but the mistakes aren't fatal. The important thing is that you're trying to move ahead. You're not standing still. Make up your mind that you will have to take some chances. Can you think of a better person to take a chance on than yourself?

This book does not cover everything you could ever possibly want to know about writing, but it will help you with expository writing—writing that explains. You won't be writing stories or poetry. You will be concentrating on the kind of writing you need in school when you have to produce a composition, or on the job when you need to produce a report, or at home when you want to explain an idea in a letter.

As with any skill you learn, once you get started, you will discover short cuts and tricks to make your writing better. Practice the ones that produce the best results and share them.

Are you ready? Let's begin our journey slowly. Don't be in a hurry. Take time to enjoy each step forward that you make.

1. Some Tricks of the Trade

All of us, whether we're beginning writers or very experienced writers, face the same problems whenever we have to write. We are faced with a blank sheet of paper. Often, just looking at that blank page and knowing that we have to fill it with something that makes sense can be overwhelming. To some of us it is almost paralyzing, and we are ready to stop even before we begin.

If you often feel this way when you have to write something, you're in good company. Ernest Hemingway, the famous author who wrote such beautiful novels as *The Old Man and the Sea* and *A Farewell To Arms*, used to feel the same way. In another of his books, *A Moveable Feast*, he told about how, early in his career, he would have to give himself pep talks before he could write:

> "...sometimes when I was starting a new story and I could not get it going, I would sit in front of the fire and squeeze the peel of the little oranges into the edge of the flame and watch the sputter of blue that they made. I would stand and look out over the roofs of Paris and think, 'Do not worry. You have always written before and you will write now'..."

Later in that same book, he talked about how hard it was for him to write and how time-consuming it was:

> "... writing had been wonderful to do. But it was very difficult, and I did not know how I would ever write anything as long as a novel. It often took me a full morning of work to write a paragraph."

Of course, he finally did write those novels, but it took time and patience. People who are good writers have taken the time and effort to learn the skill. While you may never become as great a writer as Hemingway, you, like Hemingway, will have to move step by step through the learning process to become the best writer you can be.

Whenever you feel discouraged at how long it takes to write anything good, remember that other people have felt exactly the same way. Even people who have become great writers have stood in the same spot you stand in today—at the beginning of a long journey. Use Hemingway's trick. Give yourself a pep talk, and get on with the task of learning—of moving ahead. You, too, can succeed.

Let me share with you a couple of other tricks I find helpful whenever I feel like quitting before I even begin writing. One trick I find useful is to take a few minutes to step back and take a look at where I want to go and the best route I can take to get there. I get oriented. I think about how a basic composition should look. I get a picture of what I am aiming for.

An Overview of a Basic Composition

On the next page is a model of a basic composition. You will notice that it contains four paragraphs. Each paragraph contains four or five sentences.

Take a few minutes to examine each part of the model carefully. After you examine it, I will tell you about each part in more detail. Right now, however, just study it so that you will have a picture of the model in your mind as you write. It will help to keep you moving in the right direction.

This model will also help you to get over the feeling that your writing task is never going to end. With the model before you, you can see your progress as you compose the material for each of the four sections, and the task of writing won't seem as endless.

Composition Model 1

Introduction

Sentence 1 ____
______________________________. *Sentence 2* _______
__________________________. *Sentence 3* __________.
Thesis statement ___________________________________
________________________.

First Major Idea

Topic sentence _______________________________.
Sentence 2 ______________________. *Sentence 3* ___
_____________________________. *Sentence 4* _________
_______________________. *Sentence 5* ______________
____.

Facts
Examples
Incidents
Reasons

Second Major Idea

Topic sentence _______________________________.
Sentence 2 ______________________________________.
Sentence 3 ______________________. *Sentence 4* ___
_________________________________. *Sentence 5* _______
____.

Facts
Examples
Incidents
Reasons

Conclusion

Sentence 1 _________________. *Sentence 2* _________
___________________________. *Sentence 3* ____________
____________________. *Sentence 4* __________________.

Close your eyes. Can you picture this model in your head? If you can, you're ready to go on. If not, study the model a little longer.

Now let's look at each section more carefully and determine the function of each of these parts. We will discuss how to write them later. For now, let's be sure that we understand:

- what each section does and
- how each section is related to the other parts.

Introduction

The first section of a basic composition is the *Introduction*. This is where you acquaint your reader with the subject you are writing about and try to get your reader interested in what you have to say. To do this you may tell a brief story or use a quote that relates to your topic, or you might provide some background information on your topic.

The last sentence in the Introduction is labeled the *thesis statement*. This is the sentence in the composition which states what the composition is about. It is the most important sentence in the composition since it explains the exact subject of the entire composition. Here is an example:

Thesis statement: There are two important reasons for learning to write well.

When readers look at the thesis statement, they know what to expect. They know that the composition is not about antique automobiles or the benefits of a college education. They expect to read about the reasons for learning to write well. Now it is up to the writer to meet the reader's expectations. The writer must discuss why it is important to learn to write well and not stray off onto other topics. We will discuss how to write good thesis statements later.

First Major Idea

The second section of the composition is called the *First Major Idea*. Here you develop your thesis statement by presenting detailed information that tells your reader about your topic.

Notice that this section begins with a *topic sentence*. Just as a thesis statement tells the reader what the entire composition is about, the topic sentence states what that particular paragraph is about.

Using our same thesis statement, the First Major Idea section might begin with the topic sentence below.

Thesis statement: There are two important reasons for learning to write well.

Topic sentence 1: One reason is that learning to write well will help others to understand our ideas better.

The rest of the paragraph following the topic sentence would use *facts, examples, incidents*, or *reasons* to explain how learning to write well will help others to understand our ideas better. Here are brief definitions of these terms.

Facts: specific pieces of information such as names, dates, numbers, or statistics. Facts are used to support your ideas.

Examples: short descriptions of particular items or situations. Examples illustrate your ideas.

Incidents: longer descriptions of events which have happened to you. Incidents also illustrate ideas.

Reasons: explanations of why you believe or do something. Reasons are used to support your ideas.

Later, we will examine how to use facts, examples, incidents, and reasons to develop a paragraph. For now, it is important for you to see that the First Major Idea section is directly tied to the thesis statement because the topic sentence makes a statement which supports or explains the thesis statement.

Second Major Idea

This part of the composition serves the same purpose as the First Major Idea section. It develops the thesis statement. Like the First Major Idea section, the Second Major Idea section begins with a topic sentence. The topic sentence is developed or explained by using facts, examples, incidents, or reasons. Using the same thesis statement as before, let's look at a possible topic sentence for this section of the composition.

Topic sentence 2:	Another reason is that learning to write well will help us to understand ourselves better.

The remainder of this section of the composition would develop or explain the second reason it is important to learn to write well—to help us to understand ourselves better.

Like the First Major Idea section, this part of the composition is directly related to the thesis statement because the topic sentence states an idea which supports or explains the thesis statement. If we put this topic sentence together with the thesis statement and the first topic sentence, the composition begins to take some shape.

Thesis statement:	There are two important reasons for learning to write well.
Topic sentence 1:	One reason is that learning to write well will help others to understand our ideas better.
Topic sentence 2:	Another reason is that learning to write well will help us to understand ourselves better.

Let's take this thesis statement and the two topic sentences and put them into our composition model. Take a look at the model on the next page and see how each of these sentences fits into the composition pattern. We will examine what to put in the rest of the composition later.

Composition Model 2

Introduction

Sentence 1 ______________________________ ______________. *Sentence 2* ______________________ ______. *Sentence 3* ______________________________ ____.

Thesis statement: There are two important reasons for learning to write well.

First Major Idea

Topic sentence 1: One reason is that learning to write well will help others to understand our ideas better. *Sentence 2* ______________________. *Sentence 3* ______ ______________________________. *Sentence 4* ______ ____________________. *Sentence 5* ______________ ______________________________________.

Second Major Idea

Topic sentence 2: Another reason is that learning to write well will help us to understand ourselves better. *Sentence 2* ______________________________ ______________________. *Sentence 3* ______________ ______________________. *Sentence 4* ______________. *Sentence 5* ______________________________.

Conclusion

Sentence 1 ______________________. *Sentence 2* ______ ______________________________. *Sentence 3* ________ __________________. *Sentence 4* ______________________.

Conclusion

The last section of our model is the *Conclusion*. This doesn't have to be anything fancy. What you are trying to do in this section is to summarize your ideas, tying them all together, so that you and your reader will have a sense that you have completed your thoughts. We will discuss some techniques for writing good conclusions in Chapter 6.

Expanding the Model

This model shows only two Major Idea sections. If you want to write a longer composition, you would have more paragraphs developing more major ideas, or you might devote several paragraphs to developing one major idea. It depends on your purpose for writing. For most topics, you should develop at least two major ideas.

Chapter Summary

After carefully examining the composition model, you can see that a composition has order to it. It has a *beginning*, where the writer introduces the subject. It has a *middle*, which explains and develops ideas about the subject. Our model has only two paragraphs in this section. As you become more experienced and want to add more ideas, you will add more paragraphs. When you are starting out, however, two paragraphs in this section are fine. Finally, a composition has an *ending* where the writer ties together all the ideas.

The trick is to keep this model in your mind as you write. The task, then, won't seem so overwhelming. You know that you have to write a beginning, a middle, and an ending.

* * *

Now that you know where you are going, you need to take all those ideas you have floating around in your head and place them into the section where they belong. That's the next trick of writing I want to share with you.

2. Five Steps to Writing

Now that you know where you are going, you need to know the best route to take you there. You have seen the model of a composition, and now you want to try to produce your own composition. You need to know what to put into the four parts of the model. This, of course, is the part that often seems so overwhelming to most of us.

One reason that writing often seems a bigger task than we care to tackle is that we try to do everything at once. We try to come up with the ideas, write them down in an organized fashion, and make absolutely no mistakes—all at the same time. Let me share a secret with you. Even experienced writers can't do all those things at the same time. It takes them a long time to produce a piece of writing that is good because they have to go through exactly the same process you do. Sure, they can do it a little faster than you do and maybe the results are better, but they have practiced more than you have.

Do you remember, as a little child, trying to tie your shoes? You'd sit and watch how smoothly and quickly the adults around you tied their shoes. But when you tried, it seemed to take forever, if you could do it at all. Eventually you did learn to tie your shoes, and today you do it without even thinking. But you had to learn. You had to practice, taking the task step by step, until you combined all the steps into one smooth, effortless action.

You've done the same thing with a million other tasks that you have learned to do since you were young. Do you remember learning to ride a bike? When you grew up, you progressed to more sophisticated learning tasks. As an adult, you learned to drive a car, which took some time and practice. Do you remember learning to make a right turn in the car? According to a driving instructor I talked with, you need to go through 10 steps in order to make a right turn:

1. When approaching for a right turn, check the traffic conditions.
2. Use the proper hand or automotive signal for a right turn at the distance indicated in your state regulations.
3. When the way is clear, move to the right edge of the roadway.
4. While giving the signal, apply the brake until the car is about 30 feet from the intersection.
5. Check for traffic signs or lights, pedestrians, and obstructions.
6. Take your foot off the brake and discontinue your hand signal, if you are using one.
7. Keeping your right foot poised over the brake pedal, turn the corner slowly using the hand-over-hand steering technique.
8. Enter the street as close as possible to the right edge of the roadway.
9. When power is needed to keep the car moving, gradually step on the accelerator as the front wheels are straightened.
10. Increase your speed to a safe level.

The first time you tried to put all those steps together, you may have gone too wide or scraped the curb. But you practiced. You repeated each step over in your head as you performed it rather awkwardly at first, then more smoothly and efficiently.

Writing is no different from any of these other skills that you've mastered in your life. You must trust yourself enough to know you have the ability to learn to write, just as you had the ability to learn to tie your shoes or drive a car.

The key is to break down the large task into small tasks. First you do step one, then step two, and so on until you have the task completed. At first, you may feel clumsy and hesitant, the way you did when you first tried to tie your shoes. But as you practice each step, the process will come easier, and you will be quicker and more efficient. The secret is in taking it one step at a time and practicing.

This is another trick of the trade. Think of writing as a step-by-step process. It then becomes something you can handle because you don't have to think about everything at once. You take one step at a time.

My five steps to writing are:

1. Think
2. Develop a thesis statement
3. Plan organization and development
4. Write
5. Edit

As you see, it's not a very long list—fewer steps than it takes to make a right turn. And it's not anything you can't handle if you don't try to do everything at once. Just take one step at a time.

Some of the steps take more time than others, but don't be discouraged. Learning to write well, like learning to do anything well, takes time.

Now let's take a quick look at each of the five steps to writing. In the chapters which follow, we will explore each of these steps in detail. I'll show you how each of them helps you to develop your composition.

Step 1. Think

The first and most important step is the thinking step. Stop to consider the reason anyone writes anything. It's the same reason people read anything—for ideas. People write because they have something to say—information to convey, an opinion to express, a feeling to explain, an insight to share. People read because they need or want to know things—facts, people's opinions, people's feelings, all sorts of information.

In order for the writing to be good, the thinking has to be good. If you don't have anything to say, you don't have anything to write. It's as simple as that. If your ideas are good and if your thinking is clear, your writing will be good. The spelling and punctuation can always be fixed. But it doesn't work the other way around. No matter how good the spelling and punctuation are, if the ideas aren't there, the writing won't be good.

Your first task in becoming a writer, then, is to be a thinker. Ask yourself some questions. What am I writing about? What are my ideas on this subject? How do I feel about this? Have I read anything about this? Questions like these will start seeds of ideas growing, and the all-important thinking process will begin.

In the next chapter, we will practice some techniques which will help us to generate ideas to write about. For now just remember that this is the first step in the writing process, and it is the most critical.

Step 2. Develop a Thesis Statement

In Chapter 1, we looked at a model of a composition. The first paragraph contained a thesis statement. As we saw in the first chapter, this is the sentence in your composition which focuses the reader's attention on the specific subject that you want to develop.

When you go through Step 1, the thinking stage of your writing, you will find that you have a great many ideas to write about. In a short composition, however, there is no way to do justice to all of them. You have to pick and choose what you want to focus on. The thesis statement gives a clear sense of what you will be writing about.

We will discuss how to write effective thesis statements in Chapter 4. Just remember that this is the single most important sentence in your composition, since it tells the reader exactly what you are writing about. It is a promise you are making to the reader that this is the subject you are about to explore together.

Step 3. Plan Organization and Development

Once you have promised your reader what you are going to write about, you decide how best to support or explain your thesis statement. This is the point in the composition process where you decide on the ideas to include and the best method to develop those ideas.

You can now pick and choose ideas that fit your thesis statement from the thinking you did in Step 1. You select the ideas to put into the First Major Idea and the Second Major Idea sections of the composition. You also decide what methods of development will best make your ideas clear to the reader. Should you use facts, examples, incidents, or reasons, or a combination of these to make your points clear and vivid to your reader? The decisions you make here will be based on the thinking session where lots of ideas poured from your mind.

Step 4. Write

You'll notice that we are already at Step 4, and we haven't started to write a composition yet. We've been thinking and focusing on what we want to say and deciding the best method to use to make our ideas clear to our reader. These are important steps because they are going to make the actual writing of the composition much easier. Many writers fail to go through all the preliminary steps and then wonder why writing is so hard. The reason is that they don't know where they are going or how to get there.

Once you have completed the first three steps, you have a plan in front of you. Basically, you already know what you want to say, so you can concentrate on getting it all down on paper without worrying about losing any of your wonderful ideas.

When you reach this step, use the plan that you have set up and just write. Don't worry about spelling, punctuation, grammar, or any of those things that usually concern you so much. The important thing at this stage is to get the ideas down on paper. Just push on and write, write, write! You don't have to think about any of those other things until you are satisfied that you have all your ideas down on paper.

In this step, all you do is write. No worrying is allowed. Simply concentrate on developing those great ideas you have.

Step 5. Edit

At this point, you'll have a composition in front of you. It is your rough draft. You have your ideas down on paper. The hardest part is over. You've formed an idea inside your head, then brought it out into the world and given it some form and shape. The last step is to polish your presentation.

You check your thesis statement to see if it reflects what your composition is about. Then you check your topic sentences to be sure they relate to your thesis statement. Next you check to be sure you have adequately developed your ideas in support of your thesis statement and topic sentences. You look at what you wrote to see that it is what you meant to communicate. Then you revise what you wrote to make it clearer to the reader.

Next you check for technical problems and fix them. You look for trouble spots such as misspelled words, punctuation problems, incomplete sentences, sentences which run together, and usage problems.

In Chapter 8, we will discuss some of the most common technical errors writers make, and you will be put on alert to look for them in your own writing. This takes a little practice, but it is basically a matter of recognizing them and then fixing them.

Chapter Summary

That's it. There aren't a million things to think about at one time. You need to remember only five steps that you take one at a time as you work on a composition.

Step 1 is to think about your subject and to come up with good ideas related to it.

Step 2 is to develop a thesis statement so that your reader will know exactly what to expect.

Step 3 is to select major ideas and to decide where to place them, and then to plan the best method to use to develop them—facts, examples, incidents, or reasons.

Step 4 is to write without worrying about anything, simply getting your ideas down on paper.

Step 5 is the step in which you go back over your work and edit it.

* * *

In the next chapters, we will examine each of these steps in detail and give you a chance to practice each one. You won't produce a masterpiece at first, but it will be a beginning. It will be like the first time you tied your shoes or made a right turn in the car. The bow may be a little crooked or the car may scrape the curb, but with practice you will get better and better.

3. Examining Step 1: Thinking

In the last chapter I said that people read for ideas, and that is what we will concentrate on in this section—how to generate some ideas to write about.

First, you need to get over the feeling that you have nothing to say or that what you have to say wouldn't be of interest to anybody. Think about it. You know you have all sorts of ideas floating around inside you. Aren't there times (particularly when you are trying to go to sleep) when you can't turn off your mind because it is so filled with things to think about? Also, when you talk with friends or family, you have opinions on all sorts of topics from music to politics to fashion.

Furthermore, your ideas are interesting because you see the world from a unique viewpoint based on who you are, where you come from, and where you are going. No one else has had the particular combination of experiences that makes up the total you. No one else has grown up thinking exactly the same thoughts or having exactly the same feelings about things that you have had. When you share those thoughts and feelings, then they are interesting because they reflect your unique viewpoint.

When it comes to ideas, the raw material of writing, you have a gold mine inside your head. Be confident that you can and will dig out those nuggets. You need to relax and to trust yourself. Ideas flow naturally when we don't feel pressured.

If we approach the writing task as a pressure situation, we are defeated before we begin. It is exactly that feeling of being pressured that can make writing so difficult for many of us. When we worry about whether a teacher will like what we have to say, or whether the composition will be long enough, or whether our poor spelling will make us look foolish, all is lost. That kind of worrying drains us of our energy, and we have nothing left to actually create with.

And that is exactly what writing is—creating. You shape and mold something out of what is inside you—out of your ideas, your insights, your impressions. You are a powerful creator. Creating is basic to good writing, and it is the first kind of thinking that you need to do. Once you understand that you have the power already inside you to create a piece of writing, the other steps fall into place just as they did when you learned to drive a car. Once you had the confidence, all you needed was practice.

To get started, simply jump in. Don't waste your time and your creative energy worrying about anything. Take all that energy and focus it on the task of digging out the ideas you have inside you and putting them down on paper.

Brainstorming—What Is It?

One of the best techniques I have found for digging out these ideas is called *brainstorming*. It is a simple technique that allows you almost magically to locate ideas in your head and transfer them to your paper.

Brainstorming is like a free association game you played as a kid when you sat on the back steps with your friends on a hot summer evening enjoying a cherry Popsicle. Remember? Your friend would say, "What's the first word that comes to you when I say *red*?" And you would reply "light" or "Riding Hood" or whatever you associated with the word *red*.

Try it now. What is the first thing you think of when you read a word like *job*...or *music*...or *childhood*? That's all there is to it. Brainstorming is just that, except you do it with pencil and paper, and you do many associations for each word.

Brainstorming—How to Do It

1. Find a nice quiet spot where you won't be disturbed for a while, so that your mind can wander and find what you need. It will. Relax and let the magic happen.
2. Take a fresh sheet of paper and write the composition topic across the top of the paper. Then calmly pause to consider it.
3. Before long, an idea will come to you. It always does; trust me. Write it down—just a few words will do. Soon another idea will come. Write it down, too. Then there will be another idea, and another. You will find that one idea will stimulate others. As your mind picks up speed, there will be a flurry of ideas. Write them *all* down. At this point, you are simply gathering material. It is important to keep everything. Later, you will sort out all your ideas and decide which ones to use in your composition.
4. After a while you will find your mind slowing down as it exhausts the supply of ideas. The time will vary depending on the topic. At that point, you simply stop. Be sure, however, that you've allowed yourself to go through the entire cycle—starting slowly, gaining speed, getting a flurry of ideas, and slowing down.

Some Brainstorming Exercises

Let's try this brainstorming technique a few times. I'll give you some composition topics, and you go through the process I have just outlined. Use a fresh sheet of paper for each topic.

There is no right or wrong in brainstorming. It is simply your mind searching through all of your knowledge, experiences, and insights for the raw material you need to perform a certain task—in this case, writing. Enjoy the lists you produce. They may teach you things about yourself you never realized before.

Exercise Directions: For each of the topics listed below, use a fresh sheet of paper and write the topic across the top of the sheet. Allow yourself to go through the entire brainstorming cycle—starting slowly, gaining speed, getting a flurry of ideas, slowing down—for each of the exercises.

1. Things I Never Learned in School
2. My Dream Vacation
3. Little Things Mean a Lot

When you have finished this brainstorming exercise, look at the examples on the next three pages. These examples show the brainstorming one person did on these same topics. Her ideas aren't in any particular order. They were written just as they came to mind. After you have completed your three brainstorming sheets, compare them to the examples. You will notice that you may have included some of the same ideas as are in the examples, but many of your ideas may be different. I always find the differences especially interesting because they reflect the different ways people look at things—our unique viewpoints. Her brainstorming isn't any better than yours. It is simply different because you have different backgrounds and experiences.

Brainstorming: Topic 1

Topic: Things I Never Learned in School

- pacing myself
- value of friendship
- what the real world is like
- just doing something, rather than always analyzing it
- value of experimentation
- sense of self
- spelling
- some lessons aren't as important as they seem
- sense of exhilaration
- ceramics
- enjoyment of music
- respect for people
- what's really important

Brainstorming: Topic 2

Topic: My Dream Vacation

- a place with a sense of history
- museums
- travel
- London
- green space
- balance of stimulating sights and relaxed pace
- no snow
- enough money
- someone to share experiences with
- time to explore
- get a sense of routine life in a new place
- good food
- new places to discover
- time to relax and enjoy

Brainstorming: Topic 3

Topic: Little Things Mean a Lot

- walking along the beach
- sunshine in my room
- Matthew's first smile
- little things I enjoy
- fed stray kitten
- kitten purring
- took stairs instead of elevator
- lost book returned
- chance meetings
- running into Ellen
- visited Chris in hospital
- hospital stay / socks
- things people did for me
- locket Pat gave me
- letters from Carol
- phone call to Bill
- invited Sue to party
- things I did for people
- donation to day care center
- baked cookies for nursing home

Chapter Summary

Brainstorming helps you to produce lists of ideas. You won't have a composition yet, but you will have the raw materials to begin creating one. You are getting started, which is always the hardest part of any job. If you stop to think about it, it wasn't all that hard either. As a matter of fact, when you relax and trust yourself, the brainstorming cycle of starting slowly, gaining speed, getting a flurry of ideas, and slowing down becomes automatic. You'll find that the process of brainstorming gets easier each time you do it because you learn to relax and to trust your mind to locate the ideas you need. After all, since your mind stored all that information, it knows best where to find it.

Practice

If you feel that you need more practice with brainstorming, you can use the topics on the next page. Continue practicing until you feel relaxed and have a sense that the ideas are flowing freely.

You will notice that ideas come more freely with some topics than with others. That is simply because we are more interested in some things than we are in others, and our brains have stored more information on those topics. Start with the topics you feel most comfortable with. As you become more experienced, you will find that you can dig out ideas on almost any of the other topics as well. It happens only with practice, however. So be sure to continue practicing.

Save your brainstorming sheets. They can form the basis of future compositions.

When you have some experience with the technique of brainstorming, you are ready to take the next step. You will now look over all the raw material you have on your brainstorming sheet and decide exactly what it is you want to focus on and use in your composition. This is the subject of the next chapter.

More Brainstorming Topics

Directions: Select a topic and write it across the top of a blank sheet of paper. Go through the entire brainstorming cycle for each topic you select—starting slowly, gaining speed, getting a flurry of ideas, then slowing down. The blank lines at the bottom of the page are for you to add some topics that mean a lot to you.

How to have a good time without money
Why it is difficult to make decisions
How winning the lottery would change your life
What your first job taught you
How television influences you
Your worst childhood fears
Your hopes for the future
How to make winter bearable
How computers are changing your life
Your definition of success
How to learn from the mistakes of others
Why people should be proud of their ethnic heritage
Why prejudice in the U.S. is a problem
Why education is a lifelong activity
Qualities you look for in a friend or mate
Why companies should offer flexible working hours
How kids today are different from kids a generation ago
How the cost of living goes up every year
How pollution of the environment is a growing problem
How the job market is changing
How your appearance influences the way people treat you

____

____

____

____

____

____

4. Examining Step 2: The Thesis Statement

At this point in the writing process, you have before you a sheet of paper containing the raw material for your writing task. Now you need to shape some of this raw material from your brainstorming session into composition form.

The beauty of having your ideas down in front of you on this brainstorming sheet is that now you can take your time creating the composition without having to worry about losing an important idea. Some of the tension has gone out of the process. You can relax and focus your energy on building your composition. To do this, let's move to the second step of this five-step process—developing a thesis statement.

I use another trick of the trade to develop a good thesis statement. I do a little role-playing. That is, I jump from playing the role of *writer* to playing the role of *reader* for a few minutes. You might ask, "Why on earth should we do that?" That's a good question. For the answer, let's examine the role of reader.

I have always found it useful to consider most people basically lazy when it comes to the job of reading. Mind you, I didn't say the reader was stupid. I said that the reader was lazy. Think about yourself as a reader for a minute. When you pick up something to read, you don't want to have to work too hard to understand the writer's ideas. The easier it is for you to get the information, the more likely it is that you will continue to read.

What does all this add up to? It simply means that smart writers give their readers guideposts to help them find their way through the written material. You make it easy for them to know what is going to happen in the piece of writing. It is like providing your readers with a map as they journey through the unknown territory of your ideas. It makes them feel secure and comfortable to know what is about to happen and where they are going. With your readers at ease, they will venture further into what you have to say and pay more attention to the ideas you are presenting. And that is your primary purpose for writing—to convey your ideas to your readers.

When you put yourself in the role of your readers and begin to understand their needs, you help yourself to become a better writer by meeting those needs.

We have discovered that readers like guideposts to help them through the written material. As we move from one step to another in the writing process, I will discuss different kinds of guideposts that you can use to help your readers orient themselves—to make them feel at home with your writing. The first guidepost we will examine is the thesis statement.

What Is a Thesis Statement?

A *thesis statement* is a sentence which appears early in your composition that tells the reader what you are writing about. It states the main idea of the composition. If you look at the composition model which appears on page 13, you will see that the thesis statement appears as the last sentence in the Introduction. For the time being, don't worry about the sentences which come before it. We can write those later.

There is no law that says the thesis statement has to be the last sentence in the Introduction, but when you are just getting started producing compositions, it is simply easier to put it there. It helps you to keep everything organized, and it helps your reader to get oriented. As your skills improve, you might want to experiment by moving the thesis statement to another spot in the Introduction. Just remember, the purpose of the thesis statement is to help your reader know what is about to happen.

What Makes a Good Thesis Statement?

A thesis statement needs to do two things: state the subject and focus on some aspect of that subject.

Stating the Subject

Your thesis statement will state the subject of your essay. From the billions of topics there are, you are simply telling your reader that you have selected one. You are going to write about music or education or being rich. Think how happy it will make your lazy readers to know what they will be reading about!

Focusing on Some Aspect of the Subject

A good thesis statement also focuses your reader's attention on some aspect of your subject. We all know that in a short composition we could never cover everything there is to say on a topic. Your thesis statement helps to put your reader's mind at ease because it tells him what aspect of the topic you plan to cover.

For example, suppose the subject is music and you are going to focus on one aspect of music—heavy metal. You create that focus by writing a thesis statement such as "Heavy metal appeals primarily to the younger generation." The reader's attention is focused not on the huge topic of music but on one specific branch of music—heavy metal. Furthermore, from your thesis statement, the reader knows that you are going to be exploring only one aspect of heavy metal—its appeal to the younger generation.

Take another example. Let's write a good thesis statement on the topic of education. We know that we don't have the inclination or the time to write everything there is to say on the topic of education, so we must focus on some aspect of education. A good thesis statement might read, "A college education doesn't guarantee a large paycheck, but it pays off in many other ways." Take a close look at what we have said. We are *not* writing about educational testing, degree requirements, or the cost of higher education. This thesis statement tells the reader that we plan to write *only* about the benefits of a college education that don't necessarily translate into money.

The Promise a Thesis Statement Makes

Your thesis statement makes a promise to the reader that you will limit what you include in your composition. If you say you are discussing heavy metal's appeal to the younger generation, that's the topic you must stick to. Everything you say in that composition must relate to that statement. You must *not* stray into a discussion of Bruce Springsteen's career unless you can tie it to your thesis statement about heavy metal.

All this makes you a very powerful creator. You are the one who sets the limits on the length and depth of your writing. If you state that your essay will explore 18 advantages of a college education, you have made a promise to your reader to do just that. You must cover 18 advantages if you expect to be considered a good writer. You are in control of the situation.

Some Practice with Thesis Statements

Let's look at a few thesis statements to see how they control everything that will follow in a composition.

Thesis statement 1: There are three reasons I prefer to watch football rather than baseball on television.

First, play the role of the reader. After reading this thesis statement what would you expect to read about in the rest of the essay? You've got it—the three reasons I prefer watching football rather than baseball on television. Now change roles and become the writer. What will you be expected to do? Yes, you will be expected to explain not one, not two, but three reasons for preferring to watch football rather than baseball on television.

Thesis statement 2: There are two important lessons I did not learn in school.

As a reader, when you look at that thesis statement, what do you automatically want to know? Yes, you want to know what the two important lessons are. Therefore, as a writer, what will you have to cover in the essay? That's right. You'll have to discuss the two lessons. Notice also that if you decided to discuss five lessons that you did not learn in school, you could simply go back and change your thesis statement.

Thesis statement 3: There are certain advantages to being tall.

As a reader, when you look at that thesis statement, what is the question that automatically comes to mind? Exactly. You want to know what the advantages are to being tall. Therefore, the writer who has raised the question must now build the essay around discussing those advantages.

More Practice

Now that you've gotten the idea of how powerful a thesis statement is, let's work on creating a thesis statement based on some of the brainstorming you did in the last chapter. Let's also keep in mind the things we have just said about the thesis statement. It should state the subject, and it should focus on some aspect of that subject.

To create a thesis statement from a brainstorming sheet, you first think about the ideas you listed during the brainstorming session and form a general impression about the ones you consider most important. Next you write a statement about that general impression. Then you check that statement by asking if that is really what you want to write about.

On page 36, there are directions which explain how to use your brainstorming sheet to create a thesis statement. On page 37 there is a sample worksheet on the topic "Little Things Mean a Lot" for you to use as an example. Study the directions and the example before creating your own thesis statement.

Creating a Thesis Statement from a Brainstorming Sheet

1. Relax and look over the items you included on your brainstorming sheet. Think about them for a few minutes.
2. What is your reaction? What things stand out as most important to you? This reaction may come to you almost automatically, as it did when you were a child looking up at the clouds. After a minute or two, you saw a face or some other kind of shape in the clouds. Your mind will do the same thing with all the ideas you have in front of you. Certain ideas will take shape, and a pattern will emerge. Then you will begin to see the direction your composition should take.
3. Write a thesis statement based on that general impression and the ideas that are most important to you. *Be sure that you write a complete sentence.* Force yourself if you have to. Writing a complete sentence will make the vague ideas and feelings become clear and will give a definite direction to your composition. If you cannot write a complete sentence, the thought is not yet clear enough in your head to be a good thesis statement. Work at shaping it until you have a complete sentence.
4. Once you have that basic statement written down in complete sentence form, put yourself in your reader's place. What questions does your thesis statement raise? Write the questions down. Now ask yourself, "Are those the questions I want to answer? Are those the things I really want to write about?" If not, go back and rework your thesis statement until it explains exactly what you want to write about.

Thesis Statement Worksheet

Write down the composition topic.

Little Things Mean a Lot

Step 1. Look over your brainstorming material.

What is your overall reaction? What is most important to you? What would you like to write about?

a little thing someone did for me
a little thing I did for someone else
both meant a lot

Step 2. Write a thesis statement based on your reaction. Make sure you write a complete sentence.

Thesis Statement

I can think of two little things that have made a difference in my life.

Step 3. Put yourself in the reader's role. What questions will the reader have?

1. What was one thing that made a difference?
2. What was the second thing that made a difference?
3. How did they make a difference?

Step 4. Look at your thesis statement and the questions in Step 3. Is this what you want to write about? If not, rework your thesis statement or select different ideas to write about from your brainstorming sheet.

Worksheet 1

Now, get out the brainstorming sheet that you created in the last chapter on the topic "Little Things Mean a Lot." Your teacher will give you a copy of the Thesis Statement Worksheet. Go through the steps on this worksheet. The thesis statement you finally develop may be very different from the example, but that's fine. You are expressing your own unique viewpoint.

Chapter Summary

One of the important secrets to good writing is to put yourself in the reader's role. When you try to meet your reader's needs by providing guideposts such as a thesis statement, you automatically begin to be a better writer.

We provide a thesis statement for our readers to help them focus on the exact topic we will be exploring. The thesis statement not only states the subject and focuses on some aspect of the subject, but it also makes a promise to the reader. It promises that you will stick to the ideas expressed in your thesis statement. Through your thesis statement, you are the powerful creator who sets the limits on the length and depth of your writing.

Practice

If you feel that you need more practice developing thesis statements, use the list of topics on page 30 at the end of Chapter 3. You have already practiced brainstorming some of these topics. Use those ideas to develop thesis statements. Your teacher will provide you with more copies of the Thesis Statement Worksheet.

When you feel that you have had sufficient practice, move on to the next chapter. There we will discuss how to keep the promise we make to our reader in our thesis statement.

5. Examining Step 3: Organization and Development

This chapter is divided into two parts. The first part focuses on how to organize your composition. It examines the process of selecting which ideas to include in your composition and deciding where to put them.

The second part of this chapter focuses on four basic methods used to develop and fully explain your ideas: facts, examples, incidents, or reasons. There are more than these four methods for developing ideas. But these methods will serve you in most writing situations.

Organization

In the last chapter, we worked on that all-important thesis statement. That sentence tells your reader what you intend to write about. It also raises some questions in the mind of the reader. Those questions are important in helping you decide how to organize and develop the rest of your composition.

In deciding where to put the answers to the reader's questions, we need to review the basic composition model we saw on page 9 of Chapter 1.

Remember that the model composition has four major parts: the Introduction, the First Major Idea section, the Second Major Idea section, and the Conclusion. Now we need to see how some of the ideas from your brainstorming session fit into this model. Then, you'll plan the organization of your composition.

Introduction

I will explain several methods for writing an introduction in the next chapter. Right now we need to be concerned only with the *thesis statement*. That's easy. You wrote one on your Thesis Statement Worksheet. You'll use that thesis statement as the last sentence of the introduction. It will act as the first guidepost, telling the reader what the whole composition is going to be about.

First Major Idea

Next we'll turn our attention to the First Major Idea section. The first sentence in this paragraph will be the *topic sentence*. This sentence will answer one of the reader's questions on your Thesis Statement Worksheet. You will decide which question you want to answer first. Then you'll look at your brainstorming sheet to find an answer to that question. When you have found an answer that you want to use, you will write a topic sentence that tells what this paragraph will be about. This topic sentence will serve as the second guidepost for the reader.

Second Major Idea

Just as for the First Major Idea section, the first sentence you write in this section will be a *topic sentence*. It will answer another of the reader's questions on your Thesis Statement Worksheet. You will again select the answer from the ideas on your brainstorming sheet. Simple? Yes. This sentence will also provide a guidepost which tells the reader what you will be writing about in this paragraph.

Conclusion

The final section of the composition is the Conclusion. This part will come fairly easily after we have written the rest of the composition. I will explain how to write this section in the next chapter. For now, don't worry about the conclusion.

Organizing Your Composition

Now that you know generally what is supposed to go into each section of a composition, you are ready to organize your own composition. At this point you are not yet creating paragraphs. You are deciding what major ideas to include and where to put them in your composition. You will be outlining your composition. You will need three items:

- your brainstorming sheet
- your Thesis Statement Worksheet
- a copy of the Organization and Development Worksheet which your teacher will give you

Take a moment to examine this new worksheet. Notice that it has a space for the thesis statement. It also has spaces to write the topic sentences for the First Major Idea and Second Major Idea sections.

Before you begin to organize your composition, look at pages 42 and 43. Page 42 contains reduced copies of the sample brainstorming sheet from Chapter 3 and the sample Thesis Statement Worksheet from Chapter 4. On page 43, there is an example of an Organization and Development Worksheet which has been partly filled out from those two samples. Look at these samples and then follow the directions on page 44 to begin filling out your own Organization and Development Worksheet.

Brainstorming: Topic 3

Topic: Little Things Mean a Lot

- walking along the beach
- sunshine in my room
- Matthew's first smile
- little things I enjoy
- fed stray kitten
- kitten purring
- took stairs instead of elevator

#1 - lost book returned
- chance meetings
- running into Ellen

#2 - visited Chris in hospital
#1 - hospital stay / socks
#1 - things people did for me
#1 - locket Pat gave me
#1 - letters from Carol

#2 - phone call to Bill
#2 - invited Sue to party
#2 - things I did for people
#2 - donation to day care center
#2 baked cookies for nursing home

28

Thesis Statement Worksheet

Write down the composition topic.

Little Things Mean a Lot

Step 1. Look over your brainstorming material.
What is your overall reaction? What is most important to you? What would you like to write about?

a little thing someone did for me
a little thing I did for someone else
both meant a lot

Step 2. Write a thesis statement based on your reaction. Make sure you write a complete sentence.

Thesis Statement

I can think of two little things that have made a difference in my life.

Step 3. Put yourself in the reader's role. What questions will the reader have?

1. What was one thing that made a difference?
2. What was the second thing that made a difference?
3. How did they make a difference?

Step 4. Look at your thesis statement and the questions in Step 3. Is this what you want to write about? If not, rework your thesis statement or select different ideas to write about from your brainstorming sheet.

Worksheet 1

Organization and Development Worksheet

Topic: Little Things Mean a Lot

Introduction
Write your thesis statement. Be sure it is a complete sentence.

I can think of two little things that have made a difference in my life.

First Major Idea
Write the topic sentence for your first major idea. Write a complete sentence.

The first little thing is something someone did for me.

Support for first major idea (facts, examples, incidents, or reasons):

Second Major Idea
Write the topic sentence for your second major idea. Write a complete sentence.

The second little thing is something I did for someone else.

Support for second major idea (facts, examples, incidents, or reasons):

Worksheet 2

Starting the Organization and Development Worksheet

1. Fill in your topic at the top of the Worksheet.

2. Copy the thesis statement from your Thesis Statement Worksheet onto the blank lines in the Introduction section of your Organization and Development Worksheet.

    The thesis statement, "I can think of two little things that have made a difference in my life," was written on the blank lines in the Introduction section of the sample worksheet.

3. Next, look at the reader's questions on your Thesis Statement Worksheet. Decide which question you want to answer in the First Major Idea section. Then take a few minutes to look over your brainstorming sheet. Keep in mind your overall reaction on your Thesis Statement Worksheet. Mark the ideas on your brainstorming sheet that could be used to answer the first reader's question. Decide which of these ideas you want to use, and write a topic sentence for this section of your composition. Put it on the lines in the First Major Idea section of your Organization and Development Worksheet.

    In the example, the writer decided to answer the question, "What was one thing that made a difference?" first. She looked over her brainstorming sheet and chose the idea "things people did for me." She marked several ideas, such as "lost book returned," "hospital stay/socks," "locket Pat gave me," and "letters from Carol," that referred to times when people had done something for her. Then she wrote the topic sentence "The first little thing is something someone did for me." She wrote that sentence on the blank lines under the First Major Idea section of her Organization and Development Worksheet.

4. Move on to the Second Major Idea section. Go through exactly the same process you used for the First Major Idea section. Go back to the reader's questions on the Thesis Statement

Worksheet and select another question you wish to answer or explore. Mark the ideas on your brainstorming sheet that you might want to use to answer the second question. Then create a topic sentence that answers the second question.

> In our example, the question, "What was the second thing that made a difference?" is the obvious one. That question must be answered to fulfill the promise the writer made to the reader to discuss two little things that have made a difference in her life. She decided to answer the second question with the idea "things I did for people." Again, she marked several ideas, including "visited Chris in hospital," "phone call to Bill," "invited Sue to party," and others that reminded her of times when she had done something for someone else. Then she wrote her second topic sentence, "The second little thing is something I did for someone else" on the blank lines under the Second Major Idea section of her Organization and Development Worksheet.

Practice

Before you move on to planning the development of your major ideas, you should feel confident about writing topic sentences to support thesis statements. On the following page there are a few more exercises to give you practice in writing topic sentences for various thesis statements.

When you feel comfortable about writing topic sentences, you are ready to move on to the second half of this chapter. It explains how to develop and support your topic sentences.

Practice with Writing Topic Sentences

Directions: Write topic sentences which could be used to develop each of the thesis statements written below.

1. Thesis Statement: There are two ways my life would change if I won a million dollars.

   Topic Sentence 1: ______________________________

   ____

   Topic Sentence 2: ______________________________

   ____

2. Thesis Statement: There are ways to have fun without money.

   Topic Sentence 1: ______________________________

   ____

   Topic Sentence 2: ______________________________

   ____

3. Thesis Statement: There are two important qualities I look for in a friend.

   Topic Sentence 1: ______________________________

   ____

   Topic Sentence 2: ______________________________

   ____

Planning Development

Now that we have selected our major ideas and decided which paragraphs they will go into, it's time to learn more about how we can go about developing our major ideas. It's important to remember that we need to explain our ideas completely to our reader. That's the reason we are writing.

This part of the chapter gives you four basic techniques to help you to fully explain your ideas—using facts, examples, incidents, and reasons. These techniques are not new to you. In fact, you use them all the time when you are talking.

Facts

One method for developing your paragraph is to present facts which support your topic sentence. For some topics, you will find that you have some facts at your fingertips. For example, a topic sentence such as "The cost of living seems to go up every year" is one for which you could probably state facts based on your own general knowledge. You might supply facts such as the cost of a pair of jeans or the price of a hamburger and french fries this year compared to the cost last year.

For most topics, however, you may have to depend more on an outside source such as a magazine, a book, a newspaper, or a reference book like an almanac or an encyclopedia to gather the facts that you need to develop your idea. For example, "People with a high school diploma earn more money than people without one " is one topic sentence for which you would have to go to a reference book like the *Statistical Abstract of the United States*. There you could find the facts which you could use to support that statement.

While you may have books and magazines at home to help you find facts, don't be afraid to use your school or public library to find information. The reference librarians there are specially trained to help you to locate the books, magazines, or reference books that you need. They can also suggest sources that you may not have thought of.

To decide whether you can rely on your own general knowledge or whether you need to go to an outside source, put yourself in the place of a reader and ask yourself what you would want to know if you read a topic sentence like: "Residents of Alaska pay the highest taxes in the nation." As a reader, you would want to know:

1. How much do residents of Alaska pay in taxes?
2. How much do residents of other states pay in taxes?

Most of us don't have that kind of information at our fingertips, so we need to go to an outside source to find the facts we need to answer the reader's questions. As a writer, then, you would have to go to an almanac or a newspaper or magazine article about the subject to find those specific facts.

Remember that when you are providing facts you should give them in the order of importance. That will be easy to do if you put yourself in the reader's place to discover what the reader would want to know first.

Practice with Facts

Based on the topic sentence below, ask yourself what the reader would want to know. Then provide one fact based on your own experience to develop the topic. Also, name an outside source that you might use to supply some facts to develop the topic.

1. More people are enjoying sports than ever before.

   Your own experience ______________________________

   An outside source ______________________________

   ____

Now, for each of the following topic sentences, either provide facts to develop the idea based on your own experience or name outside sources which could supply the facts that you need. You may also want to go to those sources to look up the information. Don't forget to use your library and to ask the reference librarian questions.

2. It is important to eat food that is good for you.

   A. ______________________________

   B. ______________________________

3. People spend more time watching TV today than ever before.

   A. ______________________________

   B. ______________________________

4. Water pollution is one serious problem in the U.S. today.

   A. ______________________________

   B. ______________________________

5. Wearing seat belts in a car can reduce injuries.

   A. ______________________________

   B. ______________________________

6. The use of computers in the home has also increased in the past 10 years.

   A. ______________________________

   B. ______________________________

Examples

When you hear a general statement such as "Kids today are sure different than they were 30 years ago," you automatically begin trying to envision how that statement is true or false depending on whether or not you agree with it. While trying to figure out whether it is true or false, you begin thinking of specific situations to compare the older and younger generations.

For instance, if you agree, you might say that kids today are different because they have too much and they don't understand the value of money. Thirty years ago, kids were happy to get a dime to go to the store to buy some ice cream. Today, instead of a dime for ice cream, kids get forty dollars to buy designer jeans.

This type of discussion provides your reader with an example to support the point that you believe that kids today are different. In addition, you are giving the best kind of example, a specific example, because you are giving very specific details which bring your example to life. You did not simply say that kids today have more money. You mention "a dime to buy ice cream" and "forty dollars to buy designer jeans." Those phrases are specific because they create detailed mental pictures. A phrase like "more money" does not.

Practice with Examples

Look at the topic sentence below and add one specific example which would illustrate the point.

1. Winter can be more fun for people living in the North if they get involved in outdoor activities.

   A. Skiing

   B. ______________________________

When you are developing a paragraph through the use of example, you can either give several different examples to illustrate your point or use one example and develop it in great detail. You must use your judgment to decide which method will best suit the topic.

Here is some more practice. For each of the following topic sentences, list at least two examples which would help to explain or develop that topic sentence for the reader.

2. Young people can also earn money by working for others.

   A. ______________________________

   B. ______________________________

3. Some of my childhood fears resulted from bad experiences.

   A. ______________________________

   B. ______________________________

4. Older people, too, are sometimes treated unfairly in our society.

   A. ______________________________

   B. ______________________________

5. Many of today's jobs did not exist 25 years ago.

   A. ______________________________

   B. ______________________________

Incidents

Using an incident to develop a paragraph is simply telling a story to illustrate the point that you are trying to make. It is very much like using a single example to develop a topic, but an incident usually has its roots in personal experience.

A topic sentence that lends itself to this kind of development is "The way people treat us is often based on the way we dress." I would illustrate this idea by describing the time I went to the "better dress" section of a local department store dressed in my old jeans and was completely ignored by the sales clerk even though I had $200 to spend. In relating this incident, I would include many specific details to give vitality to my story.

Practice with Incidents

For each of the following topic sentences, briefly describe one incident which would help to illustrate that topic sentence for the reader.

1. I've also learned a lot from the mistakes my friends have made.

   ____

   ____

2. Moving to a new town can be difficult, too.

   ____

   ____

3. My first job taught me one important thing.

   ____

   ____

4. Another funny thing happened one Saturday night.

____

____

5. Going out to eat can be disappointing, too.

____

____

Reasons

Suppose you are writing a composition on the kinds of decisions you find hard to make. A topic sentence might be "Making important decisions about money is also difficult."

When you put yourself in the place of your reader, a natural question that comes to mind is "Why is it difficult?" As a writer, when you begin answering that question, you begin giving reasons. Your reasons might include your fear that the decision you make might not be the right one, or your feeling that you don't have enough information or experience to make the decision, or any other reasons that you find it difficult to make decisions about money.

Practice with Reasons

List two reasons which will help explain each topic sentence to the reader.

1. People should be proud of their ethnic heritage.

   A. ______________________________________

   B. ______________________________________

2. Your education should continue throughout your life.

A. ______________________________

B. ______________________________

3. Prejudice is also a problem in the U.S.

A. ______________________________

B. ______________________________

4. Companies should allow their employees to work flexible hours.

A. ______________________________

B. ______________________________

5. I think television has a strong influence on many people.

A. ______________________________

B. ______________________________

Finishing the Organization and Development Worksheet

Now it's time to fill out the rest of your Organization and Development Worksheet on the topic "Little Things Mean a Lot." To do this, you need to decide which of the techniques—using facts, examples, incidents, or reasons—will best support or explain your topic sentences. As I discuss the sample worksheet on the next page you should follow along and complete your Organization and Development Worksheet using your own ideas.

Organization and Development Worksheet

Topic: Little Things Mean a Lot

Introduction
Write your thesis statement. Be sure it is a complete sentence.

I can think of two little things that have made a difference in my life.

First Major Idea
Write the topic sentence for your first major idea. Write a complete sentence.

The first little thing is something someone did for me.

Support for first major idea (facts, examples, incidents, or reasons):

hospital stay / socks
- roommate Marian - much older
- Marian's friend visited every day
- I had appendicitis
- the friend brought me a gift one day

Second Major Idea
Write the topic sentence for your second major idea. Write a complete sentence.

The second little thing is something I did for someone else.

Support for second major idea (facts, examples, incidents, or reasons):

invited Sue to party
- Sue didn't know anyone
- I invited her to my party
- the beginning of a wonderful friendship
- she taught me how to paint - I taught her how to cook

First Major Idea Section

For the First Major Idea section, the writer of the sample wrote the topic sentence: "The first little thing is something someone did for me." There were several ideas on her brainstorming sheet that referred to things people had done for her. She decided to write about "hospital stay/socks." This idea refers to an incident which happened to her. So this section of her composition will be developed by describing this incident. Under her first topic sentence she noted specific details that she will use to describe the incident.

Now, you decide which technique—using facts, examples, an incident, or reasons—will best develop your first topic sentence. When you wrote your topic sentence, you marked certain related ideas on your brainstorming sheet. Look at those ideas. Do they seem to be reasons or examples? Do they refer to incidents? Will they need facts to support them? When you decide which technique fits your ideas best, fill in on your worksheet the ideas you will use to support or develop your first topic sentence. Try to arrange those ideas in the order in which you plan to use them.

Second Major Idea Section

For the Second Major Idea section, the writer's topic sentence was "The second little thing is something I did for someone else." She selected "invited Sue to party" from the various ideas that referred to things she had done for other people. This also refers to an incident in her life. Again, she notes specific details about that incident that she may include in her composition.

Now you need to decide which technique (facts, examples, an incident, or reasons) to use to develop your second major idea. On your worksheet, list the ideas you will use to support or develop your second topic sentence. Arrange these details in a sensible order.

You now have an outline to write from. You don't have to worry about losing any ideas or how you are going to organize or support them. You have them on your worksheet.

Your outline is a basic guide for you to follow when you write your composition. But you are not a slave to this outline. If, as you go along, you want to make a change, do so. But be sure that any material you change or add relates to your thesis statement and topic sentences.

Remember, your thesis statement and topic sentences serve as guideposts for your reader. They help to keep the pattern of your writing clear. It is best, for your first couple of tries, to follow your outline closely. As you become more experienced, you'll be able to make changes that won't hurt anything, but first get a little experience under your belt.

Chapter Summary

In the first part of this chapter, we discussed how to organize a composition. This is done by creating topic sentences to support your thesis statement. To create your topic sentences, you looked at the reader's questions on your Thesis Statement Worksheet and found answers to those questions on your brainstorming sheet. By looking at your thesis statement and considering the reader's questions, you were able to decide what material you wanted to include in each part of your composition. By asking yourself what your reader would want to know, you decided what each of your major ideas would be.

In the second part of this chapter, you planned the development of your topic sentences. You decided whether to use facts, examples, incidents, or reasons to develop your topic sentences. You wrote down the ideas you would use to support each topic sentence. By writing all these things in outline form before you begin, you make the writing process much easier because you now know where you are going and how you are going to get there.

6. Examining Step 4: Writing

Now it's time for you to write. You've done a great deal of thinking about your subject, and you've prepared your outline. Now, you simply have to trust your remarkable brain to put it all together. And trust it you should. If you've invested some time in each of the steps we've discussed, you've done a good job of preparing your brain to do some work for you. Just let it happen.

As we begin this step in the composition process, concentrate on getting your ideas down on paper. Just write what comes naturally. Don't be concerned with anything but enjoying what you are doing. We'll worry about all the technical things—spelling, usage, grammar, sentence structure, and punctuation—in the next step.

Using the outline you have created on the topic "Little Things Mean a Lot," you will write a composition. Take just a moment to review the composition model on page 9 of Chapter 1.

You will need to produce at least four paragraphs: the Introduction, the First Major Idea section, the Second Major Idea section, and a Conclusion. Get out the Organization and Development Worksheet you filled in, and begin. Just follow the directions on the next few pages.

Directions for Writing a Composition

Now you will write the first draft of your composition. After you have written it, you will probably see some ways to improve it. You want to have space on your paper to make these improvements, so either use wide-lined composition paper or skip every other line as you write.

Begin your composition by writing your title on the first line of your paper.

Introduction

You need to produce three or four sentences for your introduction in addition to your thesis statement. Remember that these sentences catch your readers' interest and give them the necessary background on your topic. If those sentences seem to come naturally to you and you feel like writing them now, go ahead and write them. Then place the thesis statement you have already developed at the end of this paragraph.

If you are not sure what to write in the three or four sentences before the thesis statement, leave some blank lines on your paper. Later in this chapter, I'll give you a few suggestions which will help you to fill in those sentences. For now, just write the thesis statement that you have already developed as the last sentence in this paragraph.

First Major Idea Section

Next, start your second paragraph by copying the topic sentence you wrote for the First Major Idea section from your Organization and Development Worksheet. Now write four or five more sentences developing that topic sentence using the facts, examples, incidents, or reasons that you listed on your outline. Make yourself write at least four sentences. Remember—don't worry about spelling or other problems. Just get your ideas down into sentences. Once you have those four or five sentences written, you have your First Major Idea paragraph completed.

Second Major Idea Section

You produce the Second Major Idea paragraph using the same method. Take the topic sentence from the Second Major Idea section of your worksheet and write that down as the first sentence of this new paragraph. Next, write four or five more sentences using the facts, examples, incidents, or reasons you listed on your outline which explain your topic sentence. Don't worry; just write.

Conclusion

The major part of your paper is now written. You have only to wrap up your ideas and give the reader the sense that you are at an end. If you feel that you can do that easily by simply summarizing your ideas in three or four sentences, write those sentences now. If you feel that you need more help, wait until you have read the suggestions for writing conclusions which appear later in this chapter.

* * *

On the next page you will see the first draft of the composition which was written from the sample outline developed in Chapter 5. You will notice that there are errors in the composition, just as there will be errors in your first draft. Don't worry about that now. They will be fixed during the editing step. You will also notice that the introduction and the conclusion have not yet been written. These will be included later, after the sections of this chapter which explain how to write introductions and conclusions.

Sample 1 — First Draft

Little Things Mean a Lot

Introduction ______________________________________

____

____

____

I can think of two little things that have made a difference in my life.

The first little thing is something someone did for me. I was in the hospital for about a week. I was sharing a room with Marian. A much older woman. Each day one of her freind's would come to visit. This woman whose name I have forgotten would spend about an hour talking with both of us. One day I mention to her that my feet were cold. Particularily at night. This was when I had apendicitus. The next afternoon she arrived carrying a small package wraped as a gift. Too my surprise the package was for me, it was a pair of wonderfuly warm socks. Even though these socks have worn thin I still keep them. Each time I open my dresser drawer and see them, I smile to myself. Remembering the small act of kindness shown to me by someone I hardly knew.

The second little thing is something I did for someone else. I invited a person I did'nt know very well to a party. Her name was Sue and she seemed rather lost and lonely because she did'nt now anyone yet, she had just started work in our office. So I asked her to a party I was having. That party was the beginning of a wonderful freindship. In the years that has followed she has helped me solve the misteries of art and I have help her solve the misteries of cooking. Today I paint pictures which hang on my walls and she cooks gormay meals that people rave about.

Conclusion ______________________________________

____

____

____

Suggestions for Writing Introductions

When you are first starting to write compositions, keep your introductions simple. Once you become familiar and comfortable with the rest of the writing process, you can experiment. Right now, you need to be concerned with two things. First, you need to get your readers interested—capture their attention so they will want to read on. Second, you must state your topic. You've already got half the job done. You have already developed a thesis statement which states the main idea of your paper. Now you need to write at least two or three sentences that get your readers interested in the topic you are about to present.

Here are three suggestions for getting your readers interested in your topic. Notice that in each example, the thesis statement is the last sentence of the introduction.

1. **Tell a brief story that relates to your topic.**

    When I was a little girl, I used to dream of being a great singer. I could see myself as rich and famous, traveling to exciting places and doing important things that would make a difference in the world. But now that I'm an adult, I realize that it's not just the big things we do in life that make a difference. I can think of two little things that have made a difference in my life.

2. **Present historical or background information, facts, or figures that lead up to your thesis statement.** Here is an example of an introduction that provides background information.

    Many people think it's the big things in life that make a difference. They have dreams of doing something big like bringing peace to the world or being the first person to explore Mars. I think, however, that it's not just the big things we do in life that make a difference. I can think of two little things that have made a difference in my life.

3. Use a direct quotation from a person or a literary source that expresses an important idea or attitude about your topic.

> Benjamin Franklin once observed, "Little strokes fell great oaks." Of course, he wasn't talking only about chopping down trees. He was talking about life. He was saying that it's not just the big things but also the small things we do that can add up to big changes. I can think of two little things that have made a difference in my life.

There are more than these three techniques to help writers produce an introduction. These three, however, will serve you in most situations. After you have had more practice, you might want to experiment with other methods, such as asking a question or using a surprising statement to capture your reader's attention and lead into your thesis statement. For now, though, keep it simple and direct.

Now read through the two paragraphs that you have written—your First Major Idea and Second Major Idea sections—and decide which one of the three suggestions best fits your composition. Then, write the number of sentences necessary to do the job. Be sure your thesis statement is the last sentence in your introductory paragraph.

Suggestions for Writing Conclusions

Your main job in a conclusion is to pull together all the strands of the composition and tie up your ideas. This is not the place to introduce new ideas. Your conclusion should give your readers the sense that you have completed the discussion of your topic and that you have successfully supported your thesis statement.

Here are examples of three ways to conclude your composition.

1. Summarize your main points and say something significant about them.

> Things that make a difference in our lives do not always seem very important at the time. Receiving a pair of socks during a hospital stay wasn't a very glamorous event. Inviting someone to a party was also a very ordinary occurrence. However, both of those small gestures made a difference in my life.

2. Look for a lesson or conclusion that flows from the ideas you have presented.

> Buying a pair of socks and inviting someone to a party are only small gestures. At the time, both these acts seemed insignificant, but they didn't turn out to be. Those socks meant a lot to me, and whenever I can, I try to pass on little acts of kindness. Inviting Sue to my party was the beginning of a friendship that has enriched us both. While it may be important to dream of doing something big in life, we also need to remember that small gestures can add immensely to our enjoyment of life.

3. Use a concluding example that emphasizes the points you've made.

> As I was standing in line at the bank the other day, I got to thinking that our lives are very much like keeping a bank account. The small things that happen, like the coins we save, can add up, making a difference. Over the years, even little things like a pair of socks or a party invitation can add a lot of interest to our lives.

As with the introduction, there are other methods for ending a composition. You might suggest a specific action your reader might take, or use an appropriate quotation that summarizes your ideas.

The method you choose will be determined by the composition you have in front of you at the time. You have to decide which method will best tie together the ideas for both you and the reader so that you both have a sense of completion after reading the composition. Trust your judgment. Once you decide which method to use, write the three or four sentences that will fill out the conclusion.

Take a few minutes now to write the conclusion to the composition that you've been working on. On the next page you will find the first draft of the sample composition with the introduction and the conclusion now added.

Chapter Summary

There you have it! If you used your outline and followed the directions, you have produced a composition. You have created something that is uniquely yours. It all began with the ideas in your head, and now you have brought them to life on paper.

To create an introduction for a composition, you can use one of the three techniques we've covered in this chapter:

- tell a brief story
- present background information
- use a quotation.

To conclude your composition, you can:

- summarize your points and say something significant about them
- present a lesson or conclusion that flows from your ideas
- use a concluding example.

Your composition should look something like the sample composition. It should contain four paragraphs, and like the sample composition, it can probably be improved. That's okay. This is only your first draft. You will improve your composition when we move on to the last step in the composition process—editing.

Sample 1 — First Draft

Little Things Mean a Lot

Many people think its the big things in life that make a differance. They have dreams of doing something big like bringing piece to the world or being the frist person to explore Mars. I thing however that its not just the big things we do in life that make a differance. I can think of two little things that have made a differance in my life.

The first little thing is something someone did for me. I was in the hospital for about a week. I was sharing a room with Marian. A much older woman. Each day one of her freind's would come to visit. This woman whose name I have forgotten would spend about an hour talking with both of us. One day I mention to her that my feet were cold. Particularily at night. This was when I had apendicitus. The next afternoon she arrived carrying a small package wraped as a gift. Too my surprise the package was for me, it was a pair of wonderfuly warm socks. Even though these socks have worn thin I still keep them. Each time I open my dresser drawer and see them, I smile to myself. Remembering the small act of kindness shown to me by someone I hardly knew.

The second little thing is something I did for someone else. I invited a person I did'nt know very well to a party. Her name was Sue and she seemed rather lost and lonely because she did'nt now anyone yet, she had just started work in our office. So I asked her to a party I was having. That party was the beginning of a wonderful freindship. In the years that has followed she has helped me solve the misteries of art and I have help her solve the misteries of cooking. Today I paint pictures which hang on my walls and she cooks gormay meals that people rave about.

Buying a pair of socks and inviting someone to a party are only small gestures. At the time, both these act seemed insignificant, but they did'nt turn out to be. Those socks meant a lot to me and whenever I can I try to pass on little acts of kindness. Inviting Sue to my party was the beginning of a freindship that has enriched us both. While it may be important to dream of doing something big in life. We also need to remember that small gestures can add imensely to our enjoyment of life.

7. Examining Step 5: Editing

We've arrived at the last step of our journey through the writing process—editing. This is the point where you look at what you have written to see how it can be improved. You are going to check the organization and development of your ideas and search out any technical problems that are making your writing appear immature. You will be polishing your work.

This is a very important step in the writing process because the appearance of your work balances the creative ideas you have presented. As I said at the beginning of this book, we often feel squeamish about writing because our writing sometimes makes us look immature on paper. Since our ideas are mature, we always want to be sure that we present them that way. Polishing your composition will insure that you do justice to your ideas—that you present them in a mature manner.

Editing Advice

The best piece of advice about editing that I can give you is this: *Give both yourself and your composition time to rest.* This means that you should get away from the composition for a while, at least for an hour or two. It's even better if you can let it rest until the next day. You will come back to it with fresh eyes and a fresh attitude. You will be able to see many things you didn't see while you were writing the first draft. If you are trying to edit immediately after writing, you will see only what you think is there. For example, suppose you meant to write the word *marched*, but instead you wrote *march* and left off the *-ed*. When you come back to your composition after a few hours, you can look at it more objectively. You are better able to look at it as a reader would see it. That's when you can spot the mistakes. That's when you'll see *march* instead of *marched.*

More Editing Advice

The second piece of advice that I've always found useful is to *edit in an organized way.* On page 79, there is an Editing Checklist which I use when I edit my work. It helps me to look at one thing at a time, so that I don't feel overwhelmed by trying to do everything at once. Your teacher will give you a copy of this checklist to use when you begin to edit your own composition.

Examples of Editing

Before you begin editing your own composition, study the editing done on the sample composition from Chapter 6. You will find the edited draft of that composition on pages 69 and 70. Notice how the writer marked her draft for the changes she wanted to make. The final draft is on page 71. See how much better it is than the first draft.

Sample 2, another example of a composition on the same topic, appears on pages 72 through 77. This sample demonstrates some additional problems with organization and development.

The first draft of Sample 2 is on page 72. On page 73 there are suggestions for improving the organization and development of that draft. Notice that at this stage we ignore technical problems like spelling. Instead, we concentrate on the thesis statement, the topic sentences, and the paragraph development.

The second draft of Sample 2, on page 74, reflects the changes made in response to those suggestions. Then, the writer concentrates on finding and correcting technical errors. These corrections have been marked on the version found on pages 75 and 76. The final draft is on page 77.

Sample 1 — Edited Draft

Little Things Mean a Lot

Many people think ~~its~~ it's the big things in life that make a ~~differance~~ difference. They have dreams of doing something big like bringing ~~piece~~ peace to the world or being the ~~frist~~ first person to explore Mars. I ~~thing~~ think however, that ~~its~~ it's not just the big things we do in life that make a ~~differance~~ difference. I can think of two little things that have made a ~~differance~~ difference in my life.

The first little thing is something someone did for me. I was in the hospital for about a week when I had appendicitis. I was sharing a room with Marian, ~~A~~ a much older woman. Each day one of her ~~freind's~~ friends would come to visit. This woman ~~whose name I have forgotten~~ would spend about an hour talking with both of us. One day I ~~mention~~ mentioned to her that my feet were cold, ~~Particularily~~ particularly at night. ~~This was when I had apendicitus.~~ The next afternoon she arrived carrying a small package ~~wraped~~ wrapped as a gift. ~~Too~~ To my surprise, the package was for me. ~~it~~ It was a pair of ~~wonderfuly~~ wonderfully warm socks. Even though these socks have worn thin, I still keep them. Each time I open my dresser drawer and see them, I smile to myself, ~~Remembering~~ remembering the small act of kindness shown to me by someone I hardly knew.

The second little thing is something I did for someone else. I invited a person I ~~did'nt~~ didn't know very well to a party. She had just started to work in our office. Her name was Sue, and ^ She seemed rather lost and lonely because she ~~did'nt now~~ didn't know anyone yet, ~~she had just started work in our office~~. ~~So~~ so I asked her to a party I was having. That party was the beginning of a wonderful ~~freindship~~ friendship. In the years that ~~has~~ have followed, she has helped me solve the ~~misteries~~ mysteries of art, and I have ~~help~~ helped her solve the ~~misteries~~ mysteries of cooking. Today I paint pictures which hang on my walls, and she cooks ~~gormay~~ gourmet meals that people rave about.

Buying a pair of socks and inviting someone to a party are only small gestures. At the time, both these ~~act~~ acts seemed ~~insignifigant~~ insignificant, but they ~~did'nt~~ didn't turn out to be. Those socks meant a lot to me, and whenever I can, I try to pass on little acts of kindness. Inviting Sue to my party was the beginning of a ~~freindship~~ friendship that has enriched us both. While it may be important to dream of doing something big in life., ~~We~~ we also need to remember that small gestures can add ~~imensely~~ immensely to our enjoyment of life.

Sample 1 — Final Draft

Little Things Mean a Lot

Many people think it's the big things in life that make a difference. They have dreams of doing something big like bringing peace to the world or being the first person to explore Mars. I think, however, that it's not just the big things we do in life that make a difference. I can think of two little things that have made a difference in my life.

The first little thing is something someone did for me. I was in the hospital for about a week when I had appendicitis. I was sharing a room with Marian, a much older woman. Each day one of her friends would come to visit. This woman would spend about an hour talking with both of us. One day I mentioned to her that my feet were cold, particularly at night. The next afternoon she arrived carrying a small package wrapped as a gift. To my surprise, the package was for me. It was a pair of wonderfully warm socks. Even though these socks have worn thin, I still keep them. Each time I open my dresser drawer and see them, I smile to myself, remembering the small act of kindness shown to me by someone I hardly knew.

The second little thing is something I did for someone else. I invited a person I didn't know very well to a party. Her name was Sue, and she had just started to work in our office. She seemed rather lost and lonely because she didn't know anyone yet, so I asked her to a party I was having. That party was the beginning of a wonderful friendship. In the years that have followed, she has helped me solve the mysteries of art, and I have helped her solve the mysteries of cooking. Today I paint pictures which hang on my walls, and she cooks gourmet meals that people rave about.

Buying a pair of socks and inviting someone to a party are only small gestures. At the time, both these acts seemed insignificant, but they didn't turn out to be. Those socks meant a lot to me, and whenever I can, I try to pass on little acts of kindness. Inviting Sue to my party was the beginning of a friendship that has enriched us both. While it may be important to dream of doing something big in life, we also need to remember that small gestures can add immensely to our enjoyment of life.

Sample 2 — First Draft

Little Things Mean a Lot

There is an old saying about people who can't see the forrest for the trees. This means that people who consentrate on looking at individual trees don't notice that all the trees together form a forrest. The opasite of this can also be true. People sometimes see only the forrest and don't notice the individual trees that make up the forrest. Little things are importent, too.

In our modren world it is becomming very apparant that to survive we must take notice of the little things that suround us. Computer students learn about "bits" and "bytes" which refer to amounts of information that are being procesed by the computer. In our sceince classes we are taught about atoms, malequles, and there parts in order to understand our enviroment. Each of these little things are designed to fit together in a certain way and acheive certain results.

Little things are also very importent when talking about how we get along with other people. A sudden glance or smile from a stranger can mean a lot. A "Mr. Yuk" sticker on a bottle of household cleaner can mean danger to a child and we all apreciate a cheerfull "good morning" from our local postman as he makes his daily rounds.

If we are to truely understand how to get along with other people, we need to pay attention to the little things in life. All of the little things we do and say can improve or harm the quality of our lifes. This is a choice we must make every day.

Sample 2 — Suggestions for Editing First Draft

Introduction: Thesis Statement

Your introduction needs to make clear the connection between the saying about the forest and trees and your thesis statement. You also need to define your thesis statement to let the reader know exactly what the composition will be about. Your thesis statement needs to focus on which aspects of the subject you will write about. Once you have revised your thesis statement, be sure that the topic sentences in the next two paragraphs relate to it.

Paragraph 2: Topic Sentence and Development

You have the right idea about using specific examples to develop your paragraph, but be sure that they adequately explain the topic sentence. In your topic sentence, you say that "to survive we must take notice of the little things that suround us." You mention some of those little things, but you need to explain their connection to the point you are making about survival. How does noticing those little things help us to survive? If you don't want to discuss survival, you need to change your topic sentence.

Paragraph 3: Topic Sentence and Development

Your topic sentence for this paragraph says that little things are important in "how we get along with other people." Your examples of "a smile from a stranger" and a "good morning from the postman" are good, but you still need to explain why these little things are important in "how we get along with other people." Also, does your other example about "Mr. Yuk stickers" have anything to do with getting along with other people? You need to show how or else you need to develop another example.

Conclusion

Your conclusion refers only to your second major idea. When you've corrected the problems with the rest of the composition, be sure that your conclusion ties up your main ideas.

Sample 2 — Second Draft

Little Things Mean a Lot

There is an old saying about people who can't see the forrest for the trees. This means that people who consentrate on looking at individual trees don't notice that all the trees together form a forrest. The opasite of this can also be true. People sometimes see only the forrest and don't notice the individual trees that make up the forrest. Like the trees in the forrest, some little things are importent because they go together to form bigger things.

When we study technology and sceince we learn that little things form the foundation for such importent things as computers and atomic energy. Computer students learn about "bits" and "bytes" which refer to amounts of information that are being procesed by the computer and these "bits" and "bytes" are the basis for the storage and retrevil of much of man's knowledge. In our sceince classes we are taught about little things like atoms and malequles, understanding about these tiny bits of matter are the basis for understanding about atomic energy.

Little acts of kindness that people do for each other can add up to a friendlier place to live. Holding open a door for an elderly shoper at the grocery store. Voluntering to serve at a chairty event are things we can do to help each other. We all apreciate a cheerfull "good morning" from our local postman as he makes his daily rounds. Each of these little things are an example of how we can make life more pleasant for each other.

Wheather learning about computers and atomic energy or being pleasant to each other. We see that little things, like trees in the forrest, are importent. When they are by themselves, little things may not seem importent but when many of them are put together we can see that they mean alot.

Sample 2 — Edited Version of the Second Draft

Little Things Mean a Lot

There is an old saying about people who can't see the ~~forrest~~ forest for the trees. This means that people who ~~consentrate~~ concentrate on looking at individual trees don't notice that all the trees together form a ~~forrest~~ forest. The ~~opasite~~ opposite of this can also be true. People sometimes see only the ~~forrest~~ forest and don't notice the individual trees that make up the ~~forrest~~ forest. Like the trees in the ~~forrest~~ forest, some little things are ~~importent~~ important because they go together to form bigger things.

When we study technology and ~~seeince~~ science we learn that little things form the foundation for such ~~importent~~ important things as computers and atomic energy. Computer students learn about "bits" and "bytes" which refer to amounts of information that are ~~being~~ ~~processed~~ processed by ~~the~~ computer~~, and~~. ~~t~~These "bits" and "bytes" are the basis for the storage and ~~retrevil~~ retrieval of much of man's knowledge. Likewise, ~~I~~in our ~~seeince~~ science classes we are taught about little things like atoms and ~~malequles,~~ molecules. ~~u~~Understanding about these tiny bits of matter ~~are~~ is the basis for understanding about atomic energy.

Little acts of kindness that people do for each other can add up to a friendlier place to live. Holding open a door for an elderly ~~shoper~~ shopper at the grocery store, ~~Voluntering~~ and volunteering to serve at a ~~chairty~~ charity event are things we can do to help each other. Also, We all ~~apreciate~~ appreciate a ~~cheerfull~~ cheerful "good morning" from our local postman as he makes his daily rounds. Each of these little things ~~are~~ is an example of how we can make life more pleasant for each other.

~~Wheather~~ Whether learning about computers and atomic energy or being pleasant to each other, ~~We~~ see that little things, like trees in the ~~forrest~~ forest, are ~~importent~~ important. When they are by themselves, little things may not seem ~~importent~~ important but when many of them are put together we can see that they mean ~~alot~~ a lot.

Sample 2 — Final Draft

Little Things Mean a Lot

There is an old saying about people who can't see the forest for the trees. This means that people who concentrate on looking at individual trees don't notice that all the trees together form a forest. The opposite of this can also be true. People sometimes see only the forest and don't notice the individual trees that make up the forest. Like the trees in the forest, some little things are important because they go together to form bigger things.

When we study technology and science, we learn that little things form the foundation for such important things as computers and atomic energy. Computer students learn about "bits" and "bytes" which refer to amounts of information that are processed by computers. These "bits" and "bytes" are the basis for the storage and retrieval of much of man's knowledge. Likewise, in our science classes we are taught about little things like atoms and molecules. Understanding about these tiny bits of matter is the basis for understanding about atomic energy.

Little acts of kindness that people do for each other can add up to a friendlier place to live. Holding open a door for an elderly shopper at the grocery store and volunteering to serve at a charity event are things we can do to help each other. Also, we all appreciate a cheerful "good morning" from our local postman as he makes his daily rounds. Each of these little things is an example of how we can make life more pleasant for each other.

Whether learning about computers and atomic energy or being pleasant to each other, we see that little things, like trees in the forest, are important. When they are by themselves, little things may not seem important, but when many of them are put together we can see that they mean a lot.

Editing Your Composition

It's time for you to get busy editing your work. Don't be discouraged if it takes a great deal of time for your first few compositions. The process will go more quickly as you become more experienced. When you practice spotting the errors, you are also learning, and you will soon avoid making those errors.

With your copy of the Editing Checklist in front of you, go through each step. If you cannot answer *yes* to all the questions on the checklist, you will need to revise your composition. Cross out the words or phrases that you want to change, and in the spaces above them, write your improvements or corrections.

Step 1 of the checklist deals with your thesis statement. Check to make sure that it states clearly what your composition is about.

In Step 2 you check your topic sentences. Is their relationship to your thesis statement clear? Do the other sentences in each paragraph relate to the topic sentence?

Then in Step 3 you check the development of your composition. Have you used specific details to develop your ideas? Have you supported your thesis statement and your topic sentences adequately? Are all your ideas in a logical order? Are there unnecessary or unrelated details? Does your introduction capture the reader's attention and lead him into your topic? Does your conclusion bring all your ideas together and make them complete?

Finally, in Steps 4 and 5 you check your composition for technical errors and make corrections. As you practice editing your work, you'll discover that you tend to make the same kinds of errors each time you write. We seem to have certain blind spots. Using the material in Chapter 8, your teacher will help you to identify the types of errors you tend to make most often. Once you become aware of your particular blind spots, you will learn to find those errors in your work. At the end of the Editing Checklist, there are some blank lines for you to make note of your particular blind spots.

Editing Checklist

1. Check Thesis Statement

_____ Is it clear?

_____ Is it what I wrote about?

2. Check Topic Sentences

_____ Can the reader see the relationship between the thesis statement and major ideas I state in my topic sentences?

_____ Can the reader see the relationship of the other sentences in each paragraph to the topic sentence?

3. Check Development

_____ Have I developed my major idea paragraphs by using specific facts, examples, reasons, or incidents which relate to the topic sentence?

_____ Have I included enough ideas to support my thesis statement and topic sentences?

_____ Do all my ideas follow one another in a logical order?

_____ Are all my details necessary?

_____ Is my introduction interesting? Does it lead into the thesis statement?

_____ Does my conclusion tie up my ideas and give a sense that the essay is complete?

4. Check Technical Errors

_____ Spelling
_____ Comma
_____ Usage
_____ Fragments
_____ Run-ons
_____ Comma Splices
_____ Agreement
_____ Transitions

5. Check/Double-Check My Particular Blind Spots

Word endings? ______________________ ______________________________________

______________________________ ______________________________________

Worksheet 4

When you have finished going through the checklist, rewrite your composition, making the changes and corrections you have indicated on your first draft. If you have many changes to make, it is a good idea to consider this a second draft and skip lines again. This will give you space to note any further changes or corrections that need to be made. Read through your corrected version, going through the Editing Checklist a second time. Note any further improvements to be made. Then write your final draft.

Now you have completed the last step of this journey through the writing process. It's a time-consuming journey. However, you have created something that reflects the dignity of your ideas and does justice to them.

What you need now is practice. Select another of the topics in Chapter 3 for which you did the brainstorming. Go through the process again: develop a thesis statement, plan organization and development, write, and edit. Through practice you will find that writing will not only become easier, it will be much more satisfying as well.

Chapter Summary

The final step in the writing process is editing your work. After you write your first draft, get away from your composition for a while. Then, using the Editing Checklist, go through your composition step by step. Identify the things in your composition that need improvement and decide how to fix them. Then write your final draft. With practice, the editing step, like all the others, will become much easier.

* * *

Chapter 8 contains material which will help you to spot and correct some common technical problems that many writers have: spelling errors, comma problems, usage errors, sentence errors, subject and verb agreement, and the lack of transitions. You probably don't have all these problems, but you should pay close attention to the sections that apply to the problems you do have.

8. Most Common Errors

The following sections briefly explore several of the most common errors many writers make. Your teacher will help you identify which of these errors you most often make. Read the sections which deal with those errors and do the exercises. Then go over them with your teacher. Learn how to identify and fix those problems in your own writing. With practice you will learn to avoid making them altogether.

Spelling

I am a bad speller. I admit it. My life has been made more complicated because I am a bad speller, but I have learned to cope with it. I had to. I am an English teacher, and there's nothing more embarrassing than having my students correct my spelling while I am writing on the blackboard. But I have survived, and I have learned a few things about coping with a spelling problem.

If you are a bad speller, you simply have to be honest and admit it. You can't hide the problem. Let me caution you that I am not saying it is okay to have spelling mistakes in your work. It is not. I am saying that you are going to have to work a little harder during the editing stage of your writing than someone who is a good speller. That is something you must accept.

There are no quick fixes for spelling problems. I can, however, make two suggestions. The first suggestion is to master the No-Excuse Spelling List that I have included in this section. It is a list of fifty basic words that you use over and over again, so you'll save yourself a great deal of time looking them up in the dictionary if you master them now. Paste them up on your bathroom mirror or on your breakfast cereal box, and learn to spell two of them each day. Do whatever you must, but learn to spell these common words. Excuses can be made for misspelling some words, but people *always* expect these words to be spelled correctly.

The second suggestion that I offer is that you purchase a good dictionary. There are even paperback dictionaries specifically made for poor spellers. For example, one dictionary that is available is *Misspeller's Dictionary* published by Simon and Schuster. Fifteen thousand words are listed the way they are usually misspelled, and then the correct spelling is given. Other misspeller's dictionaries which are available are *The Bad Spellers Dictionary* published by Random House; *How to Spell It: A Dictionary of Commonly Misspelled Words* from the Putnam Publishing Group; and *The Spelling Helper Dictionary* published by Denco International. You might find one of them helpful.

Again, using a dictionary is no quick fix, but it is the only sure way to correct your spelling mistakes. It takes a lot of time to look up all those words, but you will find that you are looking up some of the same words over and over again. These are your personal spelling blind spots. Your teacher will give you a form on which you can list these words that you use often and that you always find yourself searching for in the dictionary. If you list them on this form and check them often, you will eventually learn how to spell them.

Finally, don't be discouraged. You'll find that the more writing you do, the more your spelling will improve. Like anything else, spelling improves with practice.

The No-Excuse Spelling List

1. accept (to accept money)
2. across
3. all right
4. always
5. among
6. beginning
7. believe
8. business
9. coming
10. criticize
11. description
12. disappear
13. disappoint
14. doesn't
15. finally
16. forty
17. hoping
18. immediately
19. its (in its nest)
20. library
21. literature
22. losing
23. minute
24. necessary
25. occurred
26. omit
27. peculiar
28. perhaps
29. pleasant
30. principal (of a school)
31. probably
32. quiet (a quiet motor)
33. realize
34. really
35. receive
36. separate
37. similar
38. surprise
39. than (more than)
40. their (their house)
41. therefore
42. too (also, excessively)
43. truly
44. until
45. usually
46. weather (rainy weather)
47. Wednesday
48. who's (who is)
49. women (several women)
50. writing

The Comma

Using commas when you write is like using pepper when you cook. A little sprinkle enhances the taste of the food. Use too much pepper, and you've spoiled a good dish. When writers use commas correctly, they help to make their sentences clear and more understandable. Commas give readers a chance to pause slightly and think about what is being said. However, when writers leave commas out or sprinkle them throughout their writing for no reason, readers get confused. They usually lose the ideas because everything either begins to run together or begins to fall apart.

Some General Advice about Commas

One easy method for deciding when to use a comma is to read your sentence aloud and place a comma at any point where your voice naturally pauses. If there is a place in the sentence where there is a definite pause but not a full stop, you should probably use a comma there. When your voice comes to a full stop, you use a period.

comma = pause
period = full stop

This method is not one hundred percent foolproof. It is a good place to start, however. It will get you through most writing situations, if you do it carefully. The trick is to recognize the difference between a pause and a full stop. You can practice that by reading through a few of the paragraphs in this section and paying close attention to where your voice naturally pauses. You should find commas at those spots.

The brief section which follows examines three basic comma rules which will give you a little more direction for placing commas in your sentences. You can still test yourself by reading the sentences aloud and listening for the pauses, but these rules give you the reasons for some of the pauses.

Three Comma Rules Which Help the Reader

1. Use a comma to set off an introductory word, phrase, or clause.

This gives your readers a slight chance to pause in the sentence to get their bearings. To see if you need a comma, read your sentence aloud and listen carefully to yourself. You will automatically insert a slight pause at the end of an introductory word, phrase, or clause. You then need to insert a comma.

Examples: Yes, I think I would like more pasta.

Just before sunrise, we finally arrived home.

After all the fun we had on vacation, it was hard to get back to work.

2. Use a comma before *and, but, or, nor, for, so,* and *yet* when they join main clauses.

Don't let your eyes glaze over just because you read the term "main clauses." That simply indicates two complete ideas. You don't have to worry, however. When you read your sentence aloud, you will hear a slight pause at the point where the comma should be inserted. You can double-check whether or not to put in the comma by looking at the list of words above.

Examples: They are only young once, *so* let them enjoy themselves.

There are many rules about commas, *but* we will cover only three of them.

They are the rules you need to apply most often, *and* you can learn them through practice.

The teacher had a great many students, *yet* she gave everyone individual attention.

3. Use a comma to separate items in a series.

This is probably the only comma rule that we remember from our elementary school days when our teachers talked about apples, oranges, peaches, and pears to illustrate the rule. It is included here just as a reminder to use a comma between the items, so that the reader doesn't get confused by having apples oranges peaches and pears all running together.

Examples: The day was dark, gloomy, and rainy.

Bobby had a pair of old shoelaces, a dead frog, and two baseball cards in his pockets.

I don't know whether to order the hot fudge sundae, the strawberry shortcake, or the chocolate cake.

If you need more practice with deciding where to use commas, complete the following exercises.

Exercises

A. Practice. Insert commas as necessary in the following sentences.

1. Ideas experiences and time are the raw ingredients of good writing.
2. The brainstorming process helps us to generate ideas and it gives us the raw materials for our composition.
3. People who learn to write are those who are willing to put in the required time effort and practice.
4. When we are learning a new skill we must be willing to take some risks.
5. If writers can put themselves in the place of readers their compositions will improve greatly.
6. However I would like to know the secrets of good writing.
7. Even though it takes a lot of effort we can't give up.
8. Editing means checking for organization development and technical problems in our writing.

9. It is important for writers to edit their work but they should let their compositions rest for a while before tackling this task.
10. During the editing process the writer assumes the role of reader.

B. More Practice. Punctuate the following paragraph correctly.

Although we may get discouraged we need to remember that writing is no different from any other skill that we have learned. It may seem like a big task but it can be broken down into five steps. Those steps are thinking developing a thesis statement planning organization and development writing and editing. Work on one step at a time and then put them all together. At first what you do may seem clumsy. However you will become more efficient more confident and more skillful with practice. The secret is to take one step at a time.

Usage

Usage errors happen when the wrong word is used in the wrong place. This kind of mistake makes writing appear immature, so it is important that you eliminate this problem from your writing. Below are five basic errors that label a writer as immature. Mastering these five usage problems will help you to move toward a more adult level of writing.

Five Basic Usage Errors

1. There, their, they're

There means *a place*. The word *here* is in the word *there*. Both are places.

Example: Place the book over there on the table.

There also *points to something*.

Example: There is the book on the table.

Their shows *possession*. When you use *their*, you are showing that someone owns or possesses something.

Example: They bought their new car last month.

They're means *they are*. The apostrophe means that the *a* has been left out of the word *are*. If you are not sure that *they're* is the word you want to use, substitute *they are* to see if it makes sense.

Example: They're going to the movies tonight.

2. To, too, two

To is a preposition.

Example: He is going to the store.

Too means *also*.

Example: Bob is eating lunch, too.

Too also means *excessively*.

Example: I ate too much.

Two means the *number* 2.

Example: Two of us are going to the show.

3. Its, it's

Its shows *possession* or *ownership.*

Example: The dog wagged its tail.

Note: Unlike nouns, pronouns do *not* show possession by adding *apostrophe s* ('s).

It's means *it is.* The apostrophe means that the *i* has been left out of the word *is.* If you are not sure that *it's* is the word you want to use, substitute *it is* to see if it makes sense.

Example: It's going to be a hot summer.

4. Your, you're

Your shows *possession* or *ownership.*

Example: Place your books on the table.

You're means *you are.* The apostrophe means that the *a* has been left out of the word *are.* If you are not sure that *you're* is the word you want to use, substitute *you are* to see if it makes sense.

Example: You're a great person!

5. Accept, except

Accept means *to approve of* or *receive.*

Examples: I will accept the job.
We do not accept personal checks.

Except means *to exclude* or *make an exception of.*

Example: We were all going except Gary.

Exercise

Underline the word in parentheses which will make the sentence correct.

1. (There, Their, They're) not going to like that decision.
2. The committee will publish (its, it's) report.
3. He (accepted, excepted) my apology.
4. (Your, You're) standing on my foot.
5. (There, Their, They're) is no room for error.
6. (Its, It's) not too late to enroll for classes.
7. Don't be late for (your, you're) class.
8. I like all kinds of ice cream (accept, except) strawberry.
9. (Its, It's) (your, you're) turn to make the coffee.
10. The council members released (there, their, they're) findings last week.
11. Whenever I go (to, too, two) an Italian restaurant, I eat (to, too, two) much.
12. (Your, You're) going to be glad you decided to (accept, except) my offer.
13. I will visit (to, too, two) cities, and Gary will come along, (to, too, two).
14. (There, Their, They're) is a place for everything, and everything is in (its, it's) place.
15. When they open (there, their, they're) presents on Christmas morning, (there, their, they're) in for a pleasant surprise.

Common Sentence Errors

There are some common errors many people make when they try to write sentences. One error is writing a part of a sentence as though it were a complete sentence. This is called a fragment. Another error is running two or more sentences together as though they were a single sentence. This is called a run-on sentence. When a comma is used instead of a period to separate sentences, it is called a comma splice. This section will help you avoid these common sentence errors.

Fragments

Fragments are incomplete sentences. They leave the reader hanging in midair, waiting for the writer to finish. If one of your friends walked up to you and said:

"When I was on my way to work last night"

and then walked away, you might think your friend had finally gone off the deep end. The problem, of course, is that your friend has given you only half a thought. The rest is missing. You would expect your friend to finish the thought by saying something like:

"When I was on my way to work last night, my car broke down."

The same holds true with writing. Your readers expect you to finish your thoughts and not leave them hanging in midair. You need to write in complete sentences.

What Are Complete Sentences? A complete sentence has both a subject and a verb and forms a complete thought. If the terms *subject* and *verb* make you break out in a rash, relax. Identifying the subject and the verb in a sentence is not all that mysterious.

To find a subject, simply ask yourself *who* or *what* the sentence is about. To find a verb, ask yourself what is the *action* or *linking* word in the sentence.

For example:

The dishes fell from the top of the cupboard.

What is the sentence about? *Dishes*. That's the subject.
What is the action word in the sentence? *Fell*. That's the verb.

The coach was happy with his players.

Who is the sentence about? *Coach*. That's the subject.
What is the linking word in the sentence? *Was*. That's the verb.

Action verbs are generally easier to identify than linking verbs are because an action verb tells what the subject *does*. A linking verb tells what the subject *is*. A linking verb links the subject to the words that describe it. Linking verbs are usually some form of the verb *be*.

Finding and Fixing Fragments. One way to find a sentence fragment in your writing is to read what you have written aloud to see if it states a complete idea. If you have the same feeling that you had when you read "When I was on my way to work last night," you have written a fragment. You have not presented a complete idea. There are three questions to ask yourself if you suspect that you have written a fragment.

1. Does your sentence have a subject that tells who or what the sentence is about?

Wrong: Being careful to lock the door. The security guard continued his rounds.

Being careful to lock the door is not a sentence. It does not contain a subject.

Right: Being careful to lock the door, the security guard continued his rounds.

The fragment has been eliminated by attaching it to the complete thought which followed it. This is one common method used to fix fragments.

2. Does your sentence have a verb, an action or a linking word?

Wrong: Someday I would like to visit some European countries. Such as France and Italy.

Such as France and Italy is not a sentence. It does not contain a verb.

Right: Someday I would like to visit some European countries such as France and Italy.

Again, the fragment has been eliminated by attaching it to a complete thought.

3. **Does your sentence form a complete thought?** Phrases and clauses which begin with words like *at, by, from, in, with, after, since, once, when, during*, and *if* need to be attached to a complete thought.

Wrong: After I spend a week in Italy. I will take the train to southern France.

Notice that there is a subject, *I*, and a verb, *spend*, in the group of words *After I spend a week in Italy*. However, it is not a complete thought. What will happen after the week in Italy?

Right: After I spend a week in Italy, I will take the train to southern France.

This fragment was also eliminated by attaching it to a complete thought.

Wrong: I would like to spend a few days on the Riviera. If I could afford it.

Again, *If I could afford it* has a subject and a verb, but it doesn't form a complete thought. It can be fixed the same way the other fragments were fixed.

Right: I would like to spend a few days on the Riviera if I could afford it.

It is sometimes better to fix a fragment by changing some of the words.

Wrong: Then I would go to Paris. Hopefully spending a whole week there.

Right: Then I would go to Paris. I would hope to spend a whole week there.

Exercises

Below are some exercises on fragments. When you learn to recognize them, you will be able to find them in your own writing. Again, the easiest way to spot fragments is to read the group of words aloud. Then, ask yourself the questions:

1. Is there a subject?
2. Is there a verb?
3. Does the group of words form a complete thought?

A. Practice. Write **S** in front of each group of words below that forms a sentence. Write **F** in front of each group that is a fragment.

____ 1. Having no time to finish our packing.

____ 2. Especially where it is cold.

____ 3. If you felt that way.

____ 4. I fell asleep while we were waiting.

____ 5. On the table in the back of the room.

____ 6. We invited Barbara to go with us.

____ 7. On a very narrow curve at the top of a steep hill.

____ 8. The children ran down to the beach as soon as we arrived.

____ 9. Hoping to meet you in school again next semester.

____ 10. People riding on their bicycles.

B. More Practice. On your own paper, rewrite the fragments below, adding whatever words are necessary to transform each fragment into a complete sentence.

1. When he woke up in the morning.
2. The program, a documentary on gun control.
3. Which had obviously been rewritten.
4. Dust settling on the car.
5. At the beginning of class.
6. By the time we reached the party.
7. Where he had spent so many years.
8. From early in the morning to late at night.
9. In the middle of the argument.
10. If the boys are still sleeping.

Run-on Sentences and Comma Splices

Run-on sentences and comma splices are other common sentence errors many writers make. A run-on sentence occurs when you run two complete sentences together without any punctuation whatsoever. A similar problem occurs when you use a comma instead of a period to separate sentences. This time, however, it is known as a comma splice. Both of these errors make it difficult for your reader to understand your ideas.

Wrong: Jonathan was absolutely ready for anything he could conquer any problem that came along. *(run-on sentence)*

Wrong: Jonathan was absolutely ready for anything, he could conquer any problem that came along. *(comma splice)*

These ideas may be interesting, but they are confusing and difficult to understand. Each example contains two complete thoughts which run together. The easiest way to fix this kind of error is to create two separate sentences. You place a period at the end of the first complete thought.

Right: Jonathan was absolutely ready for anything. He could conquer any problem that came along.

There are other ways to fix this type of writing problem, but for now you will make great progress in your writing if you can simply recognize that you are writing run-on sentences or comma splices and fix them in a very direct manner. Examine the examples below for some practice.

Wrong: Danny went fishing yesterday he caught a salmon.
Right: Danny went fishing yesterday. He caught a salmon.

Wrong: We had a terrible vacation, it rained all the time.
Right: We had a terrible vacation. It rained all the time.

Exercises

A. Practice. Correct each of the following sentences by punctuating and capitalizing them correctly.

1. Learning to write is not difficult it simply takes time.
2. Constant reading can improve your vocabulary it might also improve your spelling.
3. Many great writers found writing difficult, they wrote their novels, anyway.
4. The roles of readers and writers are not that different they both involve the communication of ideas.
5. A computer can be a great help to a writer, it can't do the writer's thinking, however.
6. One of the first tasks in learning to write is learning to think once a writer can do that, the rest is easy.
7. Most people never consider taking a writing course, they think it would be too hard.
8. Mastering the basics of writing takes time the investment pays big dividends.

B. More Practice. The following paragraph contains both fragment and run-on sentence errors. On your own paper, rewrite the paragraph, eliminating the errors.

Fragments are incomplete sentences. They leave the reader hanging in midair. Waiting for the writer to finish. Run-on sentences and comma splices are other common errors they occur when two or more complete sentences are written as a single sentence. You can find these errors in your writing. If you make up your mind to look for them. When you learn to eliminate these sentence errors. You will improve your writing a great deal.

Agreement of Subject and Verb

The subject and the verb are said to be in agreement in a sentence when they are both either singular or plural. If the subject of a sentence is singular, the verb needs to be singular, too. If the subject is plural, the sentence must have a plural verb. Many writers make the mistake of writing sentences in which the subject and the verb do not agree. They write sentences like this:

1. Charles take a nap at two o'clock every day.
2. They was happy with their brand new car.

Look at sentence 1 above. First, let's find the verb in the sentence. It is the word which indicates doing or being. In sentence 1, the verb is *take*. Second, we need to find the subject, the person or thing the sentence is about. In this sentence the subject is *Charles*. Since *Charles* is singular (one person), the verb must also be singular.

We know that adding an *s* to a noun usually makes the noun plural. With verbs, however, an *s* ending usually means the verb is singular. Sentence 1 should read:

Charles takes a nap at two o'clock every day.

Now, let's look at the agreement problem in sentence 2.

They was happy with their brand new car.

First, find the verb in the sentence (the doing or being word). It is the word *was*. Next, find the subject (the who). The subject is *they*. Since *they* is plural (more than one person), the verb must be plural, too. *Was* is a singular verb. We need to use the plural form *were*. Sentence 2 should read:

They were happy with their brand new car.

Common Agreement Problems

There are two problems with agreement that many writers have. Many people have trouble making forms of the verb *be* agree with their subjects. In addition, people sometimes have trouble recognizing the true subject of the sentence. This can lead to problems with agreement, also.

Subjects with the Verb *Be*. Many people have problems with both the present tense (happening now) and the past tense (happened in the past) of the verb *be*. The following chart may help you to sort out the special agreement problems with *be*. The most common agreement errors are *you was, we was*, and *they was*. Pay special attention to these forms. If you make these errors, get into the habit of checking this chart when you edit your work.

Present Tense of the Verb *Be*

Singular Subject	Singular Verb	Plural Subject	Plural Verb
I	am	we	are
you	are	you	are
he, she, it	is	they	are

Past Tense of the Verb *Be*

Singular Subject	Singular Verb	Plural Subject	Plural Verb
I	was	we	were
you	were	you	were
he, she, it	was	they	were

Dealing with the True Subject of the Sentence. In order to know whether to use a singular or plural verb, you need to know if the subject of that verb is singular or plural. Unfortunately, it is sometimes difficult to find the subject of a sentence. Some people get confused because they think the word closest to the verb is always the subject of that verb. To be sure that you know the true subject so that your subject and verb will agree, follow the three steps listed below.

1. Find the verb in the sentence.
2. Ask yourself what or who is doing or being. This gives you the subject of that verb.
3. If the subject is singular (one), make the verb singular. If the subject is plural (more than one), make the verb plural.

Let's follow these steps using the sentence below.

The water in those rivers is very cold.

1. What is the verb in the sentence? It's *is*.
2. Look at the sentence carefully and ask yourself what is cold.

The answer, of course, is that the *water* is cold. Even though *rivers* is the word closest to the verb, it is the water in the rivers that is cold. Since *water* is a singular subject, the verb must be singular to agree. *Is* is a singular verb.

Let's determine the true subject of the verb in the sentence below, and then choose the correct verb form:

The apples on that old tree (is, are) all rotten.

1. What is the verb in the sentence? It's *is* or *are*.
2. Next, look at the sentence carefully and ask yourself what (is, are) rotten?

The answer, of course, is that *apples* (is, are) rotten. Again, the subject is not the word closest to the verb. The thing that is rotten is not the tree, but the apples. When there is more than one word that could be the subject of a verb, you need to ask yourself *who* or *what* is doing the action or being described.

3. Choose a plural verb for the plural subject *apples*. The sentence should read:

The apples on that old tree are rotten.

Five Important Notes

1. **An *s* added to the end of a verb does not make the verb plural.** That is a rule that applies to nouns. An *s* added to the end of a verb usually means that the verb is singular. You must learn to recognize the singular and plural forms of verbs.

The Present Tense of Play			
Singular		Plural	
I	play	we	play
you	play	you	play
he, she, it	play*s*	they	play

2. **The following words are always singular and therefore take a singular verb.**

each	one	nobody	someone
either	everyone	no one	somebody
neither	everybody	anyone	

Everybody was working.
Each has his own work to do.

The following words are always plural and therefore take a plural verb.

several	both
few	many

Several are doing their homework together.

3. If a verb has two subjects that are joined by *and*, the subject is considered plural. You need a plural verb.

subject 1 + *and* + subject 2 = plural verb

Your grammar *and* punctuation *are* perfect.
Melissa *and* Meredith *play* with the toys.

4. If a verb has two singular subjects that are joined by *or, nor, either/or, neither/nor*, the subject is considered singular. You need a singular verb.

or, nor
singular subject + *either/or* + singular subject = singular verb
neither/nor

Tom *or* Phil *takes* care of all the equipment.
Neither your grammar *nor* your punctuation *is* perfect.
Either Melissa *or* Meredith *plays* with the toys.

5. If a verb has two subjects, one which is singular and one which is plural, and they are joined by *or* or *nor*, the verb agrees with the subject that is nearest to it.

singular subject + *or/nor* + plural subject = plural verb
plural subject + *or/nor* + singular subject = singular verb

One novel *or* two plays meet the reading requirement.

Plays (plural) is closest to the verb. Therefore, use the plural form *meet*.

Two plays *or* one novel *meets* the reading requirement.

Novel (singular) is closest to the verb. Therefore, use the singular form *meets*. Notice the *s* at the end of the verb *meet* which makes the verb singular.

Exercises

A. **Practice**. Underline the correct form of the verb in the sentences below.

1. The cats (likes, like) liver.
2. The coach and the players (was, were) pleased with the game.
3. The size of the huge sequoias (is, are) hard to believe.
4. The high cost of repairs always (comes, come) as a surprise.
5. The gloves and the hat (is, are) the same color.
6. Neither of the drivers (was, were) hurt.
7. The old houses in this block (is, are) being torn down.
8. Neither the doctor nor the nurse (was, were) at the office.
9. Several of the listeners (has, have) telephoned the studio.
10. The scientist's report on environmental problems (is, are) very convincing.

B. More Practice. In the paragraph below, underline the correct form of each verb in parentheses.

Neither his father nor David (was, were) able to speak for several minutes. The events of the previous days had kept them both so busy that they hadn't had a chance to talk. Now, the graduation ceremony and the party (was, were) finally over, and it (was, were) quiet in the house. Each of them (was, were) lost in his own thoughts—David thinking about the future, and his father thinking about the past. Finally, without speaking a word, they smiled at each other as memories of the past and hopes for the future (was, were) mingled together in a quiet moment of pride and gratitude.

C. Even More Practice. Underline the correct form of the verb in the sentences below.

1. Either Bob or Jeff (has been, have been) here.
2. Either the meat or the potatoes (is, are) burning.
3. The chairs and the table (was, were) loaded with packages.
4. Few in this school (knows, know) about Mr. Smith's award.
5. The sale of those books (has been, have been) disappointing.
6. Everyone in the room (was, were) listening carefully.
7. Either cookies or cake (is, are) fine for dessert.
8. The decision of the umpires (was, were) hotly disputed.
9. The president and his aides (is, are) going to the meeting.
10. Either the president or his aides (is, are) going to the meeting.

Transitions

Transitions are words and phrases that a writer uses to create bridges between ideas. Transitions can provide bridges between sentences, and they can provide bridges between whole paragraphs.

When a writer makes an effort to use transitional words and phrases, he helps the reader to move very smoothly from one idea to another. By using these bridges, the reader can easily see the connection between the ideas.

Transitions between Sentences in the Same Paragraph

Below is a short paragraph which shows you how transitional words and phrases are used to show the connection between ideas in one paragraph. The transitions are in italics. By using the words *first, second, third, fourth,* and *fifth,* the writer signals the five major ideas in the paragraph.

> That's it. There aren't a million things to think about at one time. You need to remember only five steps that you take one at a time as you construct a composition. *First,* you think about your subject and generate some good ideas relating to it. *Second,* you develop a thesis statement, so that your reader will know exactly what to expect. *Third,* you plan where to place your ideas and decide the best method of development: facts, examples, incidents, or reasons. *Fourth,* you write without worrying about anything but getting all your ideas down on paper. *Fifth,* you go back over your work and edit it by finding the problems and fixing them.

Transitions between Paragraphs

In the example below, you will find transitional words which provide a bridge from the first paragraph to the second paragraph, giving the reader a smooth pathway from one idea to the next. The transitional words are in italics.

> A good thesis statement focuses your reader's attention on some aspect of your subject. We all know that in a short composition we could never cover everything there is to say on a topic. Your thesis statement tells the reader what aspect of the topic you plan to cover.
>
> *For example*, suppose the subject is music and you are going to focus on one aspect of music—heavy metal. You create that focus by writing a thesis statement such as "Heavy metal appeals primarily to the younger generation." The reader's attention is focused not on the huge topic of music but on one specific branch of music—heavy metal.

On the next page you will find a list of common transitional words and phrases. You can use this list as a quick reference guide to help you create the connections between ideas that will help your reader to understand your writing. It doesn't contain all the possible transitional words you can use, but these words will help you in most of your writing. With practice, you will learn how to use transitions effectively. The effective use of transitions is a mark of mature writing.

Transitional Words and Phrases

To Explain Ideas

for instance	specifically	thus
for example	in particular	in other words
such as	to illustrate	that is

To Count Separate Ideas

first, second, etc.	another	again
moreover	furthermore	finally
in addition	also	besides

To Compare Ideas

likewise	in the same way	similarly

To Contrast Ideas

however	but	nevertheless
on the other hand	although	otherwise
on the contrary	in contrast	yet

To Show Cause and Effect

as a result	thus	similarly
consequently	since	unless
therefore	besides	then

To Show a Time Sequence

first, second, etc.	afterward	at once
next	meanwhile	finally
then	eventually	soon
later	immediately	at last

Exercises

Fill in appropriate transitions in the following paragraphs. Refer to the words listed on page 107 if you wish. You may use a word more than once.

One trick that helps many writers is to keep in mind a model of a basic composition. The model contains at least four major sections. ____________________, there is an introduction. It should contain several sentences, including a thesis statement. ____________________, there is a section which contains the first major idea of the paper. The sentences in this section develop that idea. ____________________, there is a section developing a second major idea. ____________________, the last section of the composition model is the conclusion.

Learning to write is like learning any other skill that you have mastered in your life. ____________________, when you were young, you learned to tie your shoelaces. It was a difficult task, but you mastered it. ____________________, when you became an adult, you learned to drive a car. It took a long time to learn all of the rules and driving skills, but you did it. ____________________, learning to write means learning some rules and investing some time, but you can do that, too.

In Conclusion

As you've gone through this book, you have taken the first steps on the road to becoming a good writer. The material that we have covered together has given you the tools to write basic compositions. However, you've traveled only the first few miles, and your journey is not over. It's an important journey, so whatever happens, don't stop.

Once you have mastered the basics, I encourage you to develop your skills further. You can begin to expand your writing skills—to explore ideas more deeply, to develop your own unique style and voice, and to deal with more complex technical problems. You can also take more time to choose words that are precise and say exactly what you mean.

Bookstores and libraries have many books on writing to help you along the next leg of your journey. Seek out the resources you need and continue to move forward—learning one thing, then adding another thing, and another. Also, consider taking additional writing courses. Having other people read and react to your writing is much more helpful, encouraging, and fun than just writing for yourself. Before you know it, you'll find that you have moved a hundred miles from where you began.

Your writing is like a mirror which reflects you—your impressions, ideas, and perspectives on life. As your writing skills continue to improve, you will find that the ideas you put down on paper will be taken more seriously because they are a more accurate reflection of the person that you are.

I hope that you are also developing a sense of pride in your writing. As you continue to learn and grow, you should gain confidence in your skills and be proud of what you have achieved. Confidence and pride in your work are an unbeatable combination of feelings that can make a lot of good things happen in your life. Don't forget, however, those good things will happen only when you have the courage to take that next step.